The COCKER SPANIEL

EDITED BY
DEREK SHAPLAND

BEST of BREED

ACKNOWLEDGEMENTS

The publishers would like to acknowledge the following for help with photography: Andy Fisher (Spinnchetti gundogs); Jane Simmonds (Shenmore); Derek and Coral Shapland (Deracor); Tracy and Chelsea Herd (Quintavia); Carol West (Sheigra); Gill Moutrey (Sunzo); Christine Taylor (Lorebank); Hearing Dogs, Pets as Therapy, members of Cockers Online (www.cockersonline.co.uk): Mary Askew, Nicole Baker, Alexa Bloësch, Rachel Innes, Freya Kennedy, Beth Lucas, Helen Noakes, Claire Pearson, Cayley Turner, Emily and Aaron Walters, Lyn Pealing.
Many thanks also to David Tomlinson for his excellent photos of working Cockers.
page 3 © istockphoto.com/Emmanuelle Bonzami; page 15 © istockphoto.com/Cristina Fumi; page 57 © istockphoto.com/Mehmet Salih Guler; page 88 © istockphoto.com/Anna Bryukhanova; page 91 © istockphoto.com/James Benet; page 101 © istockphoto.com/Emmanuelle Bonzami; page 104 © istockphoto.com/Fanelie Rosier

Cover photo: © Tracy Morgan Animal Photography (www.animalphotographer.co.uk)

The British Breed Standard reproduced in Chapter 7 is the copyright of the Kennel Club and published with the club's kind permission. Extracts from the American Breed Standard are reproduced by kind permission of the American Kennel Club.

THE QUESTION OF GENDER
The 'he' pronoun is used throughout this book in favour of the rather impersonal 'it', but no gender bias is intended.

First published in 2008 by The Pet Book Publishing Company Limited
PO Box 8 Lydney Gloucestershire GL15 6YD

Reprinted 2009 and 2010 with additions
This edition published 2011

ISBN
978-1-906305-20-8
1-906305-20-X

Printed and bound in China through Printworks Int. Ltd.

CONTENTS

GETTING TO KNOW COCKER SPANIELS

Chapter 1

The Cocker Spaniel is a merry, active, sporting dog, and has a worldwide fan club. This is a breed that has so much to offer: the Cocker is a great shooting companion, a glamorous show dog, and a wonderful pet. It is not surprising that the Cocker Spaniel is one of the most popular breeds in the UK, ranking second only to the Labrador Retriever. In the USA, the Cocker (known as the English Cocker Spaniel) has a strong following, but the Americans have made a special favourite of the American Cocker Spaniel, a breed they have developed from the English-bred Cocker.

The Cocker Spaniel was bred as a working gundog, with the specific job of flushing out game and retrieving it to hand. The breed's roots remain important to this day, as they have a lasting effect on appearance and temperament. The Cocker is a

What makes a Cocker Spaniel so special?

We are now getting used to seeing Cocker Spaniels with full tails.

compact, well-balanced dog, built on sporting lines. As a family pet, he is a very handy size: Cocker males are between 39-41 centimetres (15-16 in) at the shoulder; bitches are slightly smaller. The weight is around 12.75-14.5 kg (28 to 32 lb), with males being at the top end of the scale. In the USA, Cockers are slightly bigger and heavier. It should be remembered that the Cocker Spaniel has a very healthy appetite; he can easily gain too much weight if he uses his appealing eyes to persuade his owner that he needs treats in between meals!

The beautifully shaped head, the heart-stopping eyes, and the long, silky ears are pure Cocker Spaniel, and are features that make the breed unique. The coat is flat and silky, with feathering, and comes in a wonderful range of colours. The other outstanding characteristics are the bustling movement and the ever-wagging tail. Traditionally, Cocker Spaniels had their tails docked to prevent injury when

they were working in dense cover, and consequently, docked tails became the norm, regardless of whether dogs were worked or not. Recent legislation means that docking is now prohibited unless a dog is working as a gundog, so we are now seeing Cockers with full tails.

First and foremost, the Cocker is a happy dog – happy with life and happy with his family. Typically, a Cocker will follow you around the house, eager to know what is going on, and looking for fun or excitement. A Cocker loves to share his happiness, and if that means jumping up with muddy paws, then you have to accept the attention in the spirit it was given! As well as being a merry, fun-loving dog, the Cocker has a gentle nature and seems to share his owner's moods. His large, melting eyes show every expression from sorrow to joy. This is a dog who has a bright, optimistic outlook on life; he is intelligent and adaptable, ready to work, rest and play. This is a breed that will adapt to urban

or country living, and is ready to be a family dog, living with children, or a much-loved companion for adult owners. He is happy to be the only dog in the family, or will share his life with other dogs or cats. The Cocker is also extremely loyal and will respond to all of the love and affection that he is given.

A COCKER'S NEEDS

We are lucky that the Cocker Spaniel is a relatively easy dog to care for. He needs a well-balanced diet, regular grooming, and a programme of varied exercise (see Chapter Five). Generally, the Cocker suffers few health problems and will live to a ripe old age. The average life expectancy is 10-12 years, although some may live to 15 or even 16 years of age.

The Cocker Spaniel is an active dog, and going for walks together is one of the great pleasures of owning this merry, sporting breed. The Cocker thrives on mental stimulation, so, when exercising, add variety to the expeditions, such as retrieving or search and fetch. A pet Cocker enjoys being part of family activities and likes nothing better than collecting the children from school or having a game in the local park.

If you are taking on a puppy, exercise should be tailored to fit in with his development from puppyhood to adulthood. Formal walks for a young puppy should be severely limited, as it can result in damage to bones and joints when the pup is still growing. You will need to take him out for short spells for lead training and socialisation (see Chapter Six), but do not overtire him.

Bred to be a working gundog, the Cocker needs an active lifestyle.

The show Cocker is larger and has much more feathering than Cockers bred from working lines.

The Cocker has a silky coat with feathering, so you must be prepared for regular grooming sessions. A well-groomed Cocker is a dog to be proud of, but if you allow the coat to form mats and tangles, you will have a very uncomfortable and unkempt-looking Cocker on your hands. If you plan to show your Cocker, the workload will increase accordingly, as the coat will need to be trimmed to show off the dog's conformation. (For more information on grooming, see Chapter Five.)

THE GREAT DIVIDE

Although the Cocker Spaniel was bred to be a working dog, it has developed over the years into two distinct types: the working Cocker and the show Cocker. The Breed Standard, which is the written blueprint for the breed describing the 'perfect' Cocker Spaniel, applies to all pedigree Cocker Spaniels, but the two types can appear quite different, as they are now bred for different roles. The show Cocker is bred to adhere to the Breed Standard (see Chapter 7). The working Cocker has deviated from the Standard appearance in the quest for a spaniel that can fulfil a role as a fast-moving, intelligent and highly skilled gundog.

Working Cockers look much the same as show-bred Cocker Spaniels at eight weeks of age, but, as they develop, the differences become more evident. The skull is flatter and the muzzle is more pointed. The ears tend to be shorter and they are set higher on the head. The working Cocker is smaller in size and is generally shorter in the leg and longer in the body. The overall build is strong and slender. In order to function as a working dog, the coat is more functional and weather-resistant; it is much shorter with very little feathering or fringing on the ears.

Both show and working Cockers are highly intelligent dogs, and it is therefore essential to

THE WORKING TEMPERAMENT

The temperament of working Cocker Spaniels has to be reviewed differently from show-bred Cockers. A working Cocker is bred to work, just as the name implies. He has particularly acute scenting powers and game-finding ability, and hunts with great enthusiasm, which reflects his whole attitude to life. A working Cocker is bred with highly developed hunting instincts and natural energy, which can be more than the prospective pet buyer can cope with. Whether these energies are channelled into country pursuits or into other sports, such as obedience or agility, it is essential that owners find an outlet – or frustrations will result. Working Cocker Spaniels show affectionate and charming characteristics, which may belie their desire to have their own way. As with the show type of Cocker Spaniel, it is essential that working Cockers are disciplined and trained from an early age.

A working Cocker has highly developed hunting instincts, which need to be channelled.

COCKER COLOURS

The solid colours: Black and golden.

A black Cocker with tan markings.

A liver Cocker Spaniel. This dog is bred from working lines.

provide a good, basic training programme and plenty of mental stimulation. Although it may be stating the obvious, it needs to be emphasised that the Cocker Spaniel is a dog, not a baby, and should be treated as such. The appealing bundle of fun at eight weeks of age may look as if he can do no wrong, but if a puppy is not reared properly, problems will ensue. (For more information on training, see Chapter Six.)

COCKER COLOURS

One of the great charms of the Cocker Spaniel is that you have a great range of colours from which to choose. A Cocker can be solid-coloured (also known as self-coloured) or parti-coloured,

which is the term used when there is more than one colour in the coat. Colours within the solids are black, red or golden, liver or chocolate. The mating of one solid colour Cocker Spaniel to another can produce any one of these solid colours plus black and tan or liver/chocolate and tan. The fact that the black and tan colour has two colours usually means that, when shown, it can be entered in classes for parti-colours rather than solid colours.

If the coat colour is not roan (see Parti-colours, page 12) but has flecks of colour matching the colour other than white, the coat colour is deemed to be 'ticked'. Hence, the following colours are recognised: black and white ticked, orange and white ticked,

or lemon and white ticked. All of the ticked colours may carry a tan mask and trim if both parents carry the separate gene for this marking.

Tri-colours have three colours in the coat. The most common tri-colours are: black, white and tan; blue roan and tan; liver, white and tan; and orange roan and tan.

The colours that have been described are the most common, and all are recognised by the national Kennel Club when the puppies are being registered. Sometimes breeders register Cocker Spaniels with colours such as strawberry and white, or golden and white. These are simply variations on the colours previously described, but the

PARTI-COLOURS

Parti-colours are a little more complex, and newcomers to the breed can be easily confused, so it is worth giving a full explanation. Within parti-colours there are bi-colour and tri-colours. Recognised bi-colours include: black and white, orange and white, liver and white, and sable. If the hair has a mixture of the colours, it is known as a roan. The definition of roan is: "Having a coat in which the prevailing colour is thickly interspersed with some other." Thus, there can be: blue roan, orange roan, lemon roan, and liver or chocolate roan. A lemon roan with light brown pigmentation is an extremely rare colour, as it is the most recessive of all the roans, but it is possible. Often, prospective purchasers of puppies ask for a lemon roan when really they mean an orange roan. Within each of the roan colours breeders will register the colour as being either a light or a dark colour. For instance, light blue roan will signify that while there is a mixture of black and white hairs in the roan, white is the predominant colour, making the overall appearance much lighter in colour. Generally, the darker roans are dominant in colour over the more lightly marked roans.

Orange and white.

Blue roan.

breeder is unsure exactly what colour to use. Many registrations are made using the colour that predominates. (For more information on coat colours and pigmentation, see Chapter Seven.)

VERSATILE COCKERS

Cocker Spaniels are good candidates for training, as they have a natural ability and are very responsive and willing to please. The Cocker's eternally optimistic outlook on life makes him a great family pet and an excellent working dog. Cockers have been successful career dogs, and have been trained in a number of different jobs, including: detector (or sniffer) dogs, hearing dogs for the deaf, seizure alert dogs, and therapy dogs.

DETECTOR DOGS

Detector dogs, also known as sniffer dogs, were first introduced in the late 1970s have been very successful in protecting society from the dangers of imported illegal drugs. The dogs are used by Customs and Excise services, working at ports and airports, and their success rate has been remarkable. By using their highly developed sense of smell, the dogs can sniff out drugs hidden in passengers, in baggage and in any type of vehicle.

The Cocker Spaniel is suited to this work, as he can use his natural hunting and retrieving instincts, and he is biddable and eager to please. The Cocker's high level of energy and skill means that he can carry out many searches in a fraction of the time

Chocolate liver roan – one of the more unusual tri-colour combinations.

that a human would need to perform the same task. The dogs are trained to detect the four main drug scents of heroin, cocaine, amphetamine and cannabis. Some are also capable of detecting firearms, explosives, cash, meat products and tobacco. Some of the teams specialise in searching aeroplanes and boats.

The dogs roam over the cargo and baggage all the time, hunting for certain scents. Others are used on passengers and baggage that arrive daily into the country; if the dogs detect a familiar smell, they will sit in front of the passenger or baggage and stare.

The dogs enjoy their work – to them it is a game. They never come into contact with any of the

substances and never become addicted. They search for fun and are taught that if they detect a scent, their handlers will reward them through play.

HEARING DOGS FOR DEAF PEOPLE

A hearing dog changes the life of a deaf person on many levels. Deafness can be a very isolating and lonely disability; a hearing dog can offer a practical alternative to technical equipment, with the added benefit of giving the recipient increased independence, greater confidence, companionship and a feeling of security. Many types of dogs are used, including Cocker Spaniels. All of them are easily recognisable by their

A hearing dog can change the life of a deaf person.

The Cocker Spaniel has an ideal temperament for therapy work, and is also a handy size.

distinctive burgundy jacket and lead slips, which helps to alert people to the recipient's otherwise 'invisible' disability.

All hearing dogs are trained by forming positive associations with sounds, using food, praise or toys as rewards. These are sounds that hearing people often take for granted, such as an alarm clock, a cooker timer, a doorbell, a telephone, or a baby alarm. On hearing any of these sounds, a hearing dog will seek out his deaf owner and touch him/her with a paw. When the owner asks, "What is it?" the hearing dog will lead his owner to the source of the sound.

A hearing dog is also trained to recognise danger sounds, such as a smoke alarm, a fire alarm, a carbon monoxide alarm and a burglar alarm. A hearing dog will alert his owner to these dangers or emergency sounds by touching

the person with his paw and then lying down in a special 'alert signal' to indicate danger. The recipient will immediately know that there is danger and can take the necessary action to ensure their own safety and that of the dog.

To be an effective hearing dog, a candidate needs to be sociable and relaxed in public situations, very alert and full of enthusiasm. To qualify, each canine candidate must pass three stages of training: socialisation training, advanced sound work training, and home placement training.

SEIZURE DOGS

Working Cocker Spaniels have been used in the United States as seizure dogs. These dogs are trained to help people who have seizures due to epilepsy or other conditions. They are trained to

bring the phone to the person when they have a seizure, alert someone in the house, press a special emergency alert button, or to simply stay with the owner, licking his face and helping him to come out of the seizure. After being with their partner for a period of time, most dogs will be able to predict when their partner is going to have a seizure, so the person can prepare ahead of time and reduce the danger of having a seizure. This helps to increase independence and peace of mind to the person, reducing the number of seizures for many. Seizure dogs are also known as seizure response dogs or seizure alert dogs. They can usually be identified by a backpack identifying them as such.

THERAPY DOGS (PAT DOGS)

Many Cocker Spaniels have been

Best of all, the Cocker Spaniel is a wonderful companion dog, with a temperament that is second to none.

successfully trained as therapy dogs, known in the UK as PAT dogs (Pets As Therapy). Their role is to visit hospital wards or nursing homes to enable patients to stroke and befriend them. A therapy dog must be a minimum of nine months of age and have lived with their owner for at least six months before an application is registered.

All dogs that are used for therapy work must pass a temperament assessment. The assessment checks that the dog is sociable and friendly, that he is calm and gentle when being stroked or handled, and is not over fearful of new, unexpected stimuli. A recent research paper has shown that visits from therapy dogs significantly improve mood states of people in residential and nursing settings. This was recently tested out on a group 52 people who attended day centres or lived in nursing homes. The ages of the people ranged between 62 and 95 years, and half of the group received visits from therapy dogs. All of the patients were asked to complete a questionnaire before and after the visit. The result showed a clear improvement in the mood state variables for those having met and interacted with a therapy dog.

The sociable Cocker Spaniel has proved to be very effective as a therapy dog. Many of the residents in the nursing homes and hospitals have owned Cocker Spaniels in the past, and this has stimulated their memories with positive results.

THERAPETS
In the USA, Cocker Spaniels have been used to great effect as Therapets. One hundred dogs of different breeds, including Cocker Spaniels, were trained to work in the Family Assistance centre in New York in an attempt to make life a little more bearable for those who lost parents, spouses, brothers or sisters in the terrorist attack on the World Trade Centre on 11 September 2001. Since the attack on the Twin Towers, these special, gentle-tempered dogs have provided unsung solace to the victims of the terrorism.

THE FIRST COCKER SPANIELS

Chapter 2

Although there is no conclusive proof, spaniels are believed to have originated in Spain – hence the name 'spaniel'. It is thought that a sporting gentleman who lived on the Spanish borders brought them over to England. References to spaniels, which are believed to be one of the oldest breeds, have been found in writings going back at least six centuries. Chaucer, in the 14th century, makes mention of the spaniel in *The Wife of Bath's Prologue* in which it is quoted, "For as a Spaynel she wol on him lepe". In Dr. Johannes Caius' book of 1570, it is written, "The Spaniells which findeth game on water". Further historical proof of the spaniel's existence is in a painting hanging at Chatsworth House, in Derbyshire, depicting Charles II with a spaniel, which appears to be very similar to the modern day Cocker.

In *The Sportsman Cabinet*, published in 1803, it states, "Spaniels are of two kinds, the larger springing spaniel and the smaller cocker, or as it is sometimes known, the 'cocking' spaniel". Although it is thought there were pure strains of Cocker going back to the mid 1700s, it was not until the early 1800s that the Cocker began to emerge as a type distinct to the other spaniel breeds. During this time they were primarily used for flushing woodcock and pheasant. Their small size and merry yet gentle nature enabled them to work with great enthusiasm in the dense cover that the other, larger, field spaniels could not penetrate.

The Return from Shooting by F. Wheatley R.A. 1788.

KENNEL CLUB STUD BOOK

Early history is rather incomplete, as prior to 1874 there were no official records to assist with the study of pedigrees. One of the first tasks that the founder of the Kennel Club, Sewallis Evelyn Shirley, undertook was to instigate the compilation of the stud book. He appointed Frank C.S. Pearce as editor, and this gentleman painstakingly compiled all the information available to him at the time. The first Kennel Club stud book was published in time for distribution at the Birmingham show held on 1 December 1874, and it covered the activities of shows held during the years 1859 to 1874. This first volume of the stud book gives the pedigrees, albeit some very sketchy, of 86 dogs and 64 bitches, under the heading of "Spaniels (Field, Cocker and Sussex)". At this time the Cocker Spaniel was only distinguished from the Field Spaniel by weight. If a dog was over 25 lb, it was deemed to be a Field Spaniel; if it was less than 25 lb, it was classed as a Cocker Spaniel. This caused some confusion, as a dog could be exhibited as a 'Cocker' at one show, then, the following week, the same dog, after a good breakfast, could weigh over 25 lb and therefore be exhibited as a 'Field'.

Woodcock shooting with spaniel-type dogs.

Cocker Spaniels. After J. Scott.

Between the years 1875 and 1885 there was no separate entry for Cockers in the Kennel Club stud book; they were simply entered under the heading "Field Spaniels". Between 1886 and 1892 they were classified under the heading "Field Spaniels (Other than liver coloured over 25 lb and Cockers under 25 lb)". In 1893, after much pressure from the Spaniel Club and breeders of the time, the Kennel Club relented and Cockers finally gained their place in the stud book as a separate breed. Since 1874 a stud book depicting the previous year's show winners has been produced annually, and, despite the odd anomaly, has proved invaluable in tracing the history of the Cocker Spaniel. Entry to the stud book is by right of wins at either shows or field trials, and once a dog has gained entry to the book, it is given a unique number.

In 1885 a Spaniel club covering all the spaniel breeds was formed, and Breed Standards were drawn up for each of the breeds. The idea of a club specifically for Cockers had been talked about before the Spaniel Club came into being, but there were objectors who believed there would not be enough support for such a club. Finally, in the summer of 1902, The Cocker Spaniel Club was founded. At the inaugural meeting Mr J.M. Porter was elected as president, Mr Oswald Burgess became the first secretary, and there was an initial membership of 35 people. It was declared that the aim of The Cocker Spaniel Club was to promote the breeding of Cocker Spaniels. One of the first tasks for the committee was

Rhea, a black Cocker Spaniel born in 1870, sired by Boulton's Champion Captain out of Rose.

to draw up a new descriptive Breed Standard, based on the Standards previously given by the Spaniel Club, to enable breeders to aim for a specific type. The successors of these founder members have worked tirelessly over the years to fulfil the original aims of the club.

One change to the constitution of The Cocker Spaniel Club in recent years has been to change the wording from "promoting the breeding of Cocker Spaniels" to "promote the 'well being' of Cocker Spaniels". The Cocker Spaniel Club has gone from strength to strength and in 2002 celebrated its centenary with special events held throughout the year. It now boasts 1,188 members, divided between UK membership 720, overseas membership 225, and the field trial section 243.

EARLY DEVELOPMENT

There were various strains of Cockers that can be attributed as the foundation of today's Cockers. It was from early lines belonging to Mr Footman of Lutterworth in Leicestershire that Mr Bullock founded his line. Other notable breeders were Mr Beverley, Mr Boulton, Mr Farrow, Mr Burdett, Mr Mousley and Lord Derby's strain. It was due to careful breeding from these bloodlines that the Cocker began to gain in popularity for his good looks, ability to work, and merry disposition.

In the early days, the weight limit had a very detrimental effect on the Cocker, as the bloodlines of Field, Cocker and Sussex were often intermingled – weight being the deciding factor in determining to which breed each dog was classified. More often than not, those spaniels that didn't come up to size were simply classed as Cockers. As a result, the breed suffered. Many of these 'misfit' dogs that had been classed as Cockers were weedy, untypical, long in body and low to the ground, which meant they did not have the stamina or conformation to carry out a day's work. The combination of being given their own place in the stud book, the abolishment of the weight limit in 1901, and the introduction of the new Breed Standard was the turning point for the breed. Almost immediately type began to improve, and the sturdy, short-backed Cocker began to emerge. It took many years of dedication to breed out untypical traits and stabilise the breed. It is to these dedicated breeders that we owe so much; their foresight and determination shaped the breed towards the Cocker Spaniel we know and love today.

CHAMPION OBO

The dog that has been hailed as the cornerstone of the breed was Mr Farrow's black dog, Ch. Obo, who was born on 14 June 1879. He was a rather small dog, who is described as weighing 22 lb, being 10 inches high at the shoulder, and 27 inches from the tip of his nose to the set on of tail. He was very successful as a show dog and easily became a Champion, but it was as a sire that he really made his mark, as he had the ability to pass on his qualities to his progeny. Almost all the Cockers of today, both in the UK and in America, can trace their ancestry back to him. Despite Obo's success, his pedigree still remains somewhat a mystery. He was home-bred, but his breeder (who was known to be fiercely protective of his bloodlines) elected to keep the finer details of his pedigree to himself. His sire was recorded as Fred, who was by Bebb (2101), who in turn was by Old Bebb, whose pedigree goes back through Lord Derby's strain. Obo's dam was simply recorded as Betty; she was a black and tan, and it is believed that she goes back through the Beaver and Runic lines.

The great Ch. Obo (right) pictured with his sire, Fred.

The influential sire Toots (Beverley Don – Fan), pictured with Ridgeway Raca (Little Smut – Dottie).

Due to the very sketchy records kept prior to the introduction of the 1874 stud book, it is not possible to say accurately which Cocker became the first Champion. However, in this first volume, Mr Boulton's Champion Captain is recorded as the sire of Rhea, although no details of Captain's pedigree are recorded. In the 1883 stud book, five were accredited with the title of Champion: Spurgin's Ch. Rover II (52619), Ch. Squaw (10480), Ch. Lass O'Devon (10473), Ch. Solus (11635) and Ch. Fop (9297). Ch. Crown Prince was the first 'of Ware' Champion that was bred by Mr R. Lloyd.

The black dog Toots (31485) was another influential sire and a grandson of Ch. Obo. Toots was described as a true Cocker in every way: he weighed 23 lb, had a good head, was well proportioned, and stood on well-boned, straight legs. He, along with the black bitch Ridgeway Raca (a granddaughter of Ch. Obo), was the foundation of Mr Caless' Bruton strain. From these two dogs, Ch. Bruton Floss, Ch.

Bruton Victor and many other notable winners were descended.

Although Alonzo (2098) (by Spurgin's Christy (2122) and out of Floss) was thought to be the progenitor of the 'coloured Cocker', it was Braeside Bustle, born on 7 July 1894 (40689), who was recognised as the first blue roan. He was by Viceroy (black) out of Braeside Bizz (liver). His colour, as given in the stud book, was: "black and white, black and blue flecked". He, again, proved to be a dominant sire and almost all of the blue roan Cockers of today are descended from him.

In these formative years, black was the most dominant colour along with some black and tans, and others of varying shades of liver. There were very few reds and there was some debate both here and in America as to the origin of the colour. It was a colour that would crop up unexpectedly, as in the case of Rouge Bowdler and Ch. Rufus Bowdler. The colour was not looked on favourably, and the only breeders to take a serious interest in establishing it were Mr and Mrs Trinder of the Arabian strain. They

used the American import Toronto, who was known to carry the red gene, and also another imported red dog, Canadian Red Jacket, along with Ch. Rufus Bowdler in their breeding programme in order to improve the colour. They were very successful and as a result the Arabian red strain became famous not only for their colour but also their good type. The red colour started becoming popular although, with the exception of the Arabian Cockers, very few of this colour were seen in the ring. Unfortunately, the rise in demand for the colour in the 1930s and 1940s saw other, less knowledgeable breeders breed red to red purely for their colour, without any regard to type, temperament or conformation. As a result, there were very poor specimens with heavy heads and frowning expressions, large feet, poor coats and untypical Cocker temperament. It took many years for responsible breeders to undo the damage caused by those 'get rich quick' breeders and stabilise the red both in conformation and temperament.

Mr R.C. de Courcy Peele pictured
with his famous Bowdler Cockers –
eight of which were Champions.

Mrs Jamieson Higgens with
the Falconers: Chuza,
Caution, Chita, and Careful.

H.S. Lloyd with Falconers Padlock
of Ware (left) and Marcus of Akron
(middle) at Swakeley's Farmhouse.

INFLUENTIAL KENNELS

The founder of the Rivington strain, Mr C.A. Phillips, was described as one of the pioneers of the breed, and this kennel produced many Champions in both blacks and parti-colours. Mr R. de Courcy Peele's Bowdler kennel produced Champion after Champion. Possibly the black bitch Ch. Jetsam Bowdler (formerly registered as Schwab Powder) was to have the greatest influence on the breed since

Obo. She was very much a modern Cocker, being very compact, excelling in neck and shoulder, and being longer in the leg – she could only be faulted on having a light eye. She was the forerunner of the type of Cocker as we know it today.

There were many more influential kennels, such as Mr J.M. Porter's Braeside, Mr Harrington's Trumpington kennels, Mr Spencer's Doony strain, the Galtrees, Rocklyn,

Fulmer, Pinbrook, Fairholme, and Mrs Jamieson Higgens' Falconers.

Richard Lloyd established his line, based on the Beverley and Bullock strains, back in 1874, but it was not until much later that the world famous 'of Ware' affix was added. After the death of Richard Lloyd, his son H.S. Lloyd took over and campaigned the 'of Ware' dogs to great heights, six times winning Best in Show at Crufts with three

BEST IN SHOW WINNERS

Lucky Star of Ware (Joyful Joe – Wildflower of Ware).

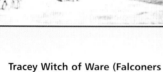

Exquisite Model of Ware (Whoopee of Ware – Janet of Ide).

Tracey Witch of Ware (Falconers Padlock of Ware – Whist).

different dogs. The first to gain this award was a blue roan called Lucky Star of Ware (813KK); he was home bred and was born on 15 September 1928. His sire was Joyful Joe (261HH), and his dam was Wildflower of Ware (923GG), and he won Best in Show two years running in 1930 and 1931. Notably, at Crufts 1931, he had to beat off the competition from a record entry of 1,006 Cockers before going on to compete against the other

breeds to win Best in Show.

The second of Mr Lloyd's dogs to achieve this award, again winning for two years in succession, 1938 and 1939, was the bitch Exquisite Model of Ware. Born on 9 July 1935, she was bred by Mr C. Youings who registered her as Brunette of Hubbastone. Her sire was Whoopee of Ware (453MM) and her dam was Janet of Ide, who was also known as Jane of Hubbastone. Next came Tracey

Witch of Ware; she won Crufts Best in Show in 1948 and also in 1950. Bred by Miss D. Weldon, she was born on 10 May 1945 and was formerly known as Witch of Tracey. Her sire was Falconers Padlock of Ware, and she was out of a bitch called Whist, who was by Lucky Star of Ware.

Like his father, H.S. Lloyd had an uncanny eye for spotting a good dog and many top winners bore his affix. When he died, the kennel fell into the care of his daughter, Jennifer Lloyd-Carey, who has also inherited her father's and grandfather's eye for a dog, and has continued to produce dogs of the type that her father would have been proud. The 'of Ware' line is unique in that it is the only kennel still in existence that has winners entered in the stud book over a period of more than 130 years.

FIELD TRIAL CHAMPIONS

The Sporting Spaniel Club held the first field trial for spaniels at Sutton Scarsdale, Chesterfield, on 3/4 January 1899; the judges being Mr W. Arkwright and Mr Elias Bishop.

The winner of the all aged stake was the Cocker Stylish Pride, owned by Mr Issac Sharpe. This young bitch also won the puppy stake at the same event.

In 1904 The Sporting Spaniel Club put on a stake confined to Cockers, and six Cockers competed. The judges were Mr R. de Courcy Peele and Mr B.C. Scammel. Beechgrove Midget won the stake with Schwab Powder (later to become Ch. Jetsam Bowdler) in second place.

In 1908 the first field trial Cocker gained her crown; she was FT Ch. Walhampton Judy (1195L) who was formerly known as Fielding Judy. Her sire is recorded as the red dog Ch. Rufus Bowdler. Nothing is known of the breeding of her dam, who was simply called Jum Jum.

The Walhampton Cockers achieved great success in the field, producing many field trial winners. The Rivington kennels were also successful in field trials as well as the show ring. Ch. Rivington Gunner gained two Certificates of Merit, thus becoming a full Champion. By 1912 the Rocklyn, Bowdler, Vivary and Doony kennels were all producing dogs that proved they still had the ability to work by winning their qualifying certificates. FT Ch. Rivington Dazzle, a son of Barnsford Brigadier, lies behind many of the early field trial Champions, and his son, FT Ch. Pat of Chishill, became known for passing his working abilities on to his progeny.

The first field trial for spaniels hosted by the Kennel Club was held in 1925, and the winner of this was the Cocker FT Ch. Elibank Attention (1674EE). His sire was Lawyette, his dam was

Influential sire FT Ch. Rivington Dazzle (left) and Rivington Rosalie.

Elibank Trixie, and he was owned and bred by Mr J. Shortt. In 1926 Mr H.S. Lloyd won the trial with the bitch Tornado of Ware (1752FF); she was by Invader of Ware out of Torment of Ware. Another 'of Ware' winner, FT Ch. Barney of Ware (1202KK), formerly known as Lick Bla Jester, won the Championship in 1930. Between the years 1940 to 1948, no field trials were held due to World War II. In 1952 there was another interruption due to an outbreak of foot and mouth disease.

Up until the 1940s show and working lines continued to be bred from the same bloodlines, but it was around this time that a split began to creep in. Those involved in the show scene were still aiming to preserve working instincts, but were concentrating on breeding good-looking and soundly constructed dogs who conformed to the Breed Standard as laid down by The Cocker Spaniel Club. The keen shooting man had no concerns for show ring looks, and based his breeding purely on working ability. As a result the 'show Cocker' and the 'working Cocker' began to evolve into two very distinct types. Sadly, by the late 1950s, the two strains had become virtually independent of

FIELD TRIAL LEADING KENNELS

One of the most notable strains of working Cocker of the last 50 years is Lt. Cdr. E.A.J. Collard's Elan kennels. His first Champion was Young Punch of Elan who was descended from FT Ch. Rivington Dazzle. Another to later make his mark on the breed was FT Ch. Buoy of Elan, whose pedigree lies behind many Championship winners. A great number of field trial Champions have emerged from this exceptionally successful kennel, to which Mr & Mrs K. Chudley's Harpersbrook line has been closely associated for many years. Other notable breeders, spanning the last 50 years, who have been influential in producing field trial Champions are: Mrs Watts (Exton), Mr T.P. Hall (Templebar), Miss P.E. Brown (Headland), Mr Keith Erlandson (Gwibernant), Mr H.C. Gwynnes (Wernffrwd), Mr Hedley Millington (Nancarrow), Dennis Douglas (Anahar), and Peter Jones (Maeswydderwen). Ian Openshaw has become well known for his skills as a handler, and he has handled many dogs to their titles.

each other. They had become two separate gene pools, with little or no breeding between the two types taking place.

FULL CHAMPIONS
In 1909 the Kennel Club introduced the qualifying certificate. This meant that before a dog could be awarded the title

of Champion, it had to pass a working test to prove that it had the ability to work in the field. The first to gain her qualifying certificate and become a full Champion was Ch. Rivington Robina. The title of Show Champion was introduced in 1958, and along with it came a new working test called the show gundog working test. As with the qualifying certificate of 1909, a dog that became a Show Champion could, if the owner so wished, take the show gundog working test in order to demonstrate the dog still had the ability to work. From this date, only those Show Champions successfully passing the working test were entitled to use the title of Champion.

After the introduction of the Show Champion title, very few owners bothered to put their dogs in for the qualifier, consequently not many Show Champions became full Champions. Among the few who did qualify for the full title were: Ch. Solinda of Traquair, Mrs K. Doxford's Ch. Broomleaf Bonny Lad of Shillwater, and Miss J. Macmillan's Ch. Lochranza Latchkey. During the 1960s other Cockers who attained this award were Mrs M. Robinson's Ch. Craigleith Cinderella and Mr A. Mansfield's Ch. Lucklena Musical Director. Mr Mansfield went on

Ch. Rivington Robena (Betham Ben – Rivington Rose).

HALL OF FAME
Cocker Spaniels who were awarded the title of Full Champion after passing a working test.

Ch. Broomleaf Bonny Lad of Shillwater (Blare of Broomleaf – Caroline of Shillwater).

Ch. Lochranza Latchkey (Treetops Foxbar Cognac – Lochranza Lottinga). Photo: Thomas Fall.

**Ch. Bournehouse Starshine
(Ch. Scoly's Starduster –
Merrybray Marie Celeste):
Winner of 60 Challenge
Certificates.
Photo: Anne Roslin-Williams.**

**Ch. Okell Outwood Bound
(Sh. Ch. Dearnewood Star
Venture – Okell Onestep).
Photo: Ian Scott.**

to train a total of five dogs to win their qualifying certificate, including Lucklena Blue Music, Light Music of Lucklena, and Lucklena Minstrel. The beautiful blue roan bitch Ch. Bournehouse Starshine, owned by Mr G. Williams, attained the award, and she also held the record for winning the highest number of show ring Challenge Certificates. She retired in 1976 after winning her 60th Challenge Certificate – a record that was not broken for many years. The Best in Show winner Ch. Ouaine Chieftain, owned by Mr & Mrs G. Caddy, Mr Schofield's Ch. Scoly's Starduster, Marion France's Ch. Peelers Cornbow Myth, and Mrs D. Owen's Ch. Saffron of Settnor all proved their working ability during the 1960s and 1970s.

In the early 1990s Danny Bowkis campaigned two of his Show Champions – Ch. Bowiskey Boy Blue and Ch. Bowiskey Island Boy – to their full titles, and around the same time Mrs J. Walker campaigned Ch. Okell Outwood Bound to his full title. Okell One For Luck and Okell Oh Boy both gained their qualifying certificates. Others to achieve their qualifying certificates were Mesdames B. Rice-Stringer and J.P. Hook's orange roan Kennelbourne Spot On, and Mrs K. Cato's blue roan dog Okell Over To You. Finally in 1993, Mrs S.V. Cox won the qualifying certificate with her blue roan dog Luchriston Quick Step.

THE COCKER IN AMERICA

The first Cocker to be registered with the American Kennel Club in 1879 was Boulton's Champion Captain. He was among the first of many who made the long journey by sea to America during these early days, and it was not long before the interest of the American breeder started to grow.

As Ch. Obo's fame spread worldwide. His owner, Mr Farrow, was approached by Mr Pitcher, a Cocker breeder in America, who tried to buy Obo. However, Mr Farrow would not part with him. It was agreed, after much persuasion, that Mr Pitcher could have a bitch called Chloe II; she was a very pretty young lady who had already proved her worth as a prize winner. Her sire was Mr Bullock's Dash, who was by Old Bebb out of the liver bitch Flirt (2101). Chloe's dam was Nellie (2225) who was by Mr Spurgin's Bebb (Young Bebb) out of Flirt (2101). In due course, Chloe II was mated to Ch. Obo and was shipped in whelp to America. The resulting litter produced Obo II, who, like his father, was able to stamp his type in his progeny, and thus became the foundation of the Obo line in America. Obo II became an American Champion and was the sire of Am. Ch. Black Duke, who in turn played his part in the foundation of the American Cocker.

The popularity of the Cocker Spaniel grew steadily in America, with breeders beginning to establish their own bloodlines. It was thought these new bloodlines, most of which carried Obo bloodlines, could be very useful to the breeders in England and this led to the import of such dogs as Toronto. Mr C.A. Phillips (Rivington) wanted to improve heads, in particular foreface, so he looked towards America for a suitable dog. The black dog Toronto, who had a combination of Obo and American blood, became one of the earliest imports. He excelled in head, and it was hoped that he would be able to pass this on and improve heads in the dogs in

Am. Ch. Obo II (Ch. Obo – Chloe II): The foundation of the breed in the USA.

England. Toronto set sail from America, but his travels were not uneventful, and, during the voyage, he became shipwrecked. However, he survived his ordeal and he went on to do exactly what was expected of him.

Following in the footsteps of Toronto, Mr Cane and Mr Lloyd imported Hampton Guard; he again carried American blood that went back through the Obo line. He was a black dog but both his parents were from red lines, so, as was expected, he carried the red gene. He was mated to Rivington Arrow, who was by Lucky Traveller, a dog with pure Field Spaniel blood, and this mating produced Ch. Rivington Rogue. Broadcaster of Ware, who also carried lines back to Obo, was imported back to England, where he also proved his worth as a sire.

Much later in the mid 1920s, Robinhurst of Ware, bred by Judge Townsend Scudder, was imported from America, again carrying original Obo blood. His sire was Robinhurst Red Rambler and his dam was Robinhurst Glosody, whose father, Robinhurst Foreglow, was born in 1921 and weighed in at 28 lb. He was considered by many to be too big and heavy, and despite his owner offering free stud services, very few breeders took up this offer. This proved to be very shortsighted, as, despite his size, this dog had much to offer. His good points far outweighed his negative points.

At this time, the Cocker in America was beginning to evolve into two distinct types: the American Cocker Spaniel as opposed to the English Cocker Spaniel. Interestingly, it was a son of Robinhurst Foreglow, Red Brucie, who was hailed as the foundation of the American Cocker Spaniel. He lived to 15 years and sired 34 American Cocker Spaniel Champions. In 1946, albeit from the same roots, the American Kennel Club considered the two types of Cocker to be sufficiently distinct in type that they became registered as two separate breeds: the American Cocker Spaniel and the English Cocker Spaniel.

Red Brucie (Robinhurst Foreglow – Ree's Dolly): The father of the American Cocker Spaniel.

TRANSATLANTIC DIFFERENCES

The difference in the English and the American-bred Cocker Spaniels resulted in a split into two distinct breeds.

The English Cocker Spaniel

The American Cocker Spaniel

COCKERS TODAY

Since the 1920s and 1930s, there have been many well-known dogs who have all done their part to shape the breed to what it is today.

Sixshot Black Swan (Treetops Terrific – Sixshot Brown Owl): Reckoned to be one of the best blacks of all time.

BLACK COCKERS

Firstly, some of the notable blacks were by Dominorum D'Arcy, who, although half parti-colour bred, sired mainly solids. He was considered to have a strong influence over the following generations of blacks. Bazel Otto, his grandson, also made his mark on the breed, and, when mated to Felbrigg Hortensia, produced Treetops Treasure Trove, the foundation of Judy de Casembroot's Treetops kennels. These kennels became world famous and dominated the awards for many years.

Also to the fore at this time was the Sixshot kennels of Mrs V. Lucas-Lucas where many top winners were produced, possibly the most famous being Sixshot Black Swan. He was another grandson of Bazel Otto and was hailed as probably one of the best black dogs of the time. Black Swan also became an influential sire; his bloodlines can be found behind most of the solid Cockers of today. Mrs K. Doxford's Broomleaf kennels were very successful, and were consistently producing Champions and top winners such as Ch. Broomleaf Bonny Lad of Shillwater, Broomleaf Black and Tan, and Sh. Ch. Broomleaf Bright Memory. Another most important kennel was Miss J. Macmillan's Lochranza, which became famous for dogs such as Sh. Ch. Lochranza Strollaway, who won 19 Challenge Certificates, and Ch. Lochranza Latchkey. Lochranza has produced many Champions over the years. Following the death of Miss Macmillan, the kennels came into the hands of John and Jean Gillespie who continue the tradition and are still producing Lochranza Champions to this day. Mrs P. Wise's Astrawin kennel produced many Champions, as did Miss D. Hahn's Misbourne kennel. Mr R. Clarke's Sh. Ch. Roanwood Ripple was a

top winner, but unfortunately she died at a young age while in whelp. Mr J. Clark's Cornbow Manfred sired many winners. Latterly, Mrs P. Lester's Quettadene Emblem, who sired eight Champions, and Mr and Mrs A. Webster's Asquanne Gonzales, the sire of 11 Champions, were both top winners who have made their mark on the breed. Finally, a mention must be made of Mr and Mrs Bentley's Sh. Ch. Canigou Cambrai who in 1996 was declared Best in Show at Crufts – the first black Cocker to achieve this award.

RED AND GOLDEN COCKERS
The popularity of the red and golden Cocker followed on from the success of the Arabian red strain as other kennels became interested in the colour. Some of the most influential reds were

Lady of Sauls, the grand dam of Woodcock Ringleader and Billy of Byfleet, both of whom had a big influence on the colour. Other kennels that added to the success of the colour were Dorswick, Aingarth, Beaunash, Bethersden, Dellcroft, Ottershaw, Rivoli, Waldiff, Hightrees, and, of course, Woodcock. Woodcock Ringleader is probably the most famous representative of this colour, closely followed by Ch. Broomleaf Bonny Lad of Shillwater. Later years saw red and golden winners from Mrs P. Trotman's Kavora kennel. From Mr and Mrs J. Smith's Sorbrook kennel came Sunglint of Sorbrook; he was most influential as a sire and features in many pedigrees. Astrawin, Lochdene, Lochranza, Broomleaf, and latterly Sh. Ch. Perrytree the Dreamer, sire of seven UK Show Champions, and his son, Sh. Ch.

Sh. Ch. Asquanne's Gonzales (Faymyr Chickadee Tan Spats – Sh Ch. Asquanne's Ghia): Sire of 11 Show Champions.

Sh. Ch. Canigou Cambrai (Sh. Ch. Cleavehill Pot of Gold – Crankwood Miss Happy): Crufts Best in Show winner 1996.

Sh. Ch. Perrytree The Dreamer (Misbourne Valdorki – Perrytree Sweet Dream): Sire of seven UK Show Champions.

Sh. Ch. Bitcon Troubador (Mistfall Meddler – Sh. Ch. Bitcon Moonlight): Sire of 14 Show Champions.

Perrytree Sun Dreamer who won 21 CCs and holds the record for a golden.

PARTI-COLOUR COCKERS

The notable parti-colours following on from Braeside Bustle and Blue Peter are Fairholme Rally, Corn Crake and Ch. Fulmer Ben – each played their part in furthering the colour. Invader of Ware was a prolific sire, siring hundreds of winners, such as Ch. Churchdene Invader and Ch. Vivary Crusader along with many others from the 'of Ware' kennel. Mrs Jamieson Higgins' strain of Falconers also had a great influence and produced many big winners. Other kennels to have great influence on the parti-colours in later years were Mrs Gold's Oxshott Marxedes, Mr A. Collins' Colinwood kennel, and Mr Richmond Weir's Weirdene kennel. Mr and Mrs Caddy's Ch. Ouaine Chieftain had a big influence, as did Mr E. Simpson's Coltrim and Mrs D. Barney's Sh. Ch. Cilleine Echelon. Mr G. Williams' Bornehouse and Mrs J. Walker's Okell were both kennels that produced dogs that also qualified in the field. Latterly, Mr and Mrs Armstrong's Bitcon Troubador proved to be a very influential dog, and sired a post-war record of 14 Champions.

BLACK AND TAN COCKERS

The black and tan, although popular during the formation years, seemed to fall out of favour and there have been very few of this colour winning top awards at shows. The first post-war winner was Broomleaf Black and Tan;

then in the 1990s Mr and Mrs Mace made up Sh. Ch. Squiersrook Duet with Fonesse. Over the last few years, the quality of the black and tan has improved tremendously, and there have been quite a number of black and tans who have gained their Junior Warrants and other top awards.

SABLE COCKERS

In recent years, the colour of sable has been added to the list of acceptable colours. It is believed the colour has been around for many years, but most breeders would have dismissed the pups as a non-Standard colour, not registered them, and given them away as pets. Reference to the sable has been found as far back as 1904 and then again in the 1930s. The first sable to be registered and shown was Ch.

Elmbury Cinnamon Teal. He was bred by Mrs Jones MBE in England, but because she didn't think English judges would like him, he was exported to Dick Squires in America. There he soon became a Champion and was found to pass his colour on to his progeny in eight out of 10 litters born. Latterly, Pam Walker of the Cardamine kennel has imported a sable dog from Germany, Navarro Sable King Vom Eshenweg (who incidentally goes back to Elmbury Cinnamon Teal) and is currently showing him and his progeny. At the present time, the colour has it critics along with its admirers.

COCKER REGISTRATIONS

In 1893, the first year that the Kennel Club recognised the Cocker as a separate breed, there were a total of 67 registered. The registration figures steadily increased over the years, and in 1914 the number had increased to 400, rising to 5,372 in 1939. By 1947 the Cocker had achieved the highest annual registration figure over all breeds, namely 27,000. 1957 saw registrations fall to 6,434 and in 1967 the figure was 5,744. In 1976 the registration system changed whereby all puppies in a litter had to be registered. Prior to this, breeders only registered the puppies in the litter that were going to be shown or worked; therefore, prior to this date, the number of registrations did not necessarily tally with the actual number of puppies born. By 1977 the figures had dropped to 2,256. In 1987, the figure had increased to 6,490; 10 years later, in 1997, the number increased to 14,541; and finally at the end of 2006 the current registration figure was 20,459.

Sh. Ch. Squiresrook Duet With Fonesse (Kendrick Surprise Surprise – Squiresrook Little Madam at Kendrick): A top-quality black and tan.

Navarro Sable King Vom Eshenweg: A sable Cocker imported from Germany.

A COCKER FOR YOUR LIFESTYLE

Chapter 3

S o, you have decided that a Cocker Spaniel is the breed for you, but are you ready for the commitment involved and have you thought about how a Cocker will fit into your lifestyle? A Cocker can live on average for 12 to 15 years, so a decision to share your life with one should not be taken lightly. Today, many people have busy lives, juggling the demands of their careers with raising young families, so careful consideration must be given to whether there is the time available to devote to a new canine member of the family.

WORK SCHEDULE
The first thing to consider is your work schedule and to assess whether this is compatible with owning a Cocker puppy or an older dog. Cockers are, by their nature, very sociable dogs who do not thrive when left alone for long periods. This is not the

Remember that a puppy is very demanding to begin with.

breed for you if you are away from home for most of the day and are unable to make arrangements for the dog to be cared for in your absence.

This is particularly true if you are thinking about buying a puppy. All puppies are very demanding in terms of the time needed for training and socialisation. A Cocker puppy will not learn to be toilet trained if there is no one at home to take him outside and teach him where to toilet, and he will quickly become bored and destructive if left to his own devices for too long.

Of course, this does not mean that owners need to be at home for 24 hours a day; it is very important that all puppies learn to be alone for short periods right from the start. However, leaving a puppy alone for eight or nine hours a day would be completely unacceptable, even if the owner was able to return home briefly at lunchtimes. Ideally, no young puppy should be left alone for longer than three hours in any one day, although this period could be increased to four hours for a well-adjusted older dog.

Some full-time workers do manage to combine their careers with owning a Cocker puppy, but it takes enormous commitment

CAN YOU AFFORD A COCKER?

Owning any dog can be expensive, so you must do your sums first and ensure you can afford not just the initial costs involved in buying a puppy but also all the ongoing costs needed to feed your dog and keep him healthy and happy for his lifetime. The initial costs will include the purchase price of a puppy together with all the start-up equipment. You also need to budget for veterinary fees, which are sometimes very high (particularly if your Cocker is ever unlucky enough to need specialist orthopaedic treatment or major surgery). Many owners take out insurance to cover such costs, but remember that pet insurance will not cover the costs of microchipping, vaccinations, worming and flea control, or routine neutering). Pet insurance is a competitive area with many companies offering varying levels of cover, so do as much research as you can to find the company offering the best cover at the most reasonable price. You may also need to pay for services such as a dog trainer, groomer, boarding kennel or dog sitter/walker.

and planning. Some are lucky enough to have reliable family members who can take care of the puppy during the working day. However, thought must still be given to contingency plans to cover holidays or periods of sickness. Other options open to the full-time worker include employing a pet sitter or a dog

walker. There are now many agencies and individuals offering such services; some are undoubtedly better than others, so it is important to check out references and ensure that adequate insurance is carried.

Such services may not be suitable for young puppies if the sitter looks after a group of dogs of varying ages. In this situation a pup could be bullied by an older dog, or he could pick up bad behavioural habits. Another possible problem is that the owner and the pet sitter may have different approaches to training dogs, which could result in a very confused puppy. A pet sitter/dog walker may therefore not be the best option for a puppy unless there is a guarantee of one-on-one attention and the sitter shares the owner's training philosophy. However, such services may be the ideal solution for someone who works full-time and has decided that an older Cocker would better suit their lifestyle. Again, the same care must be taken to ensure the owner is happy with the sitter/walker's approach to training and with the number of dogs in their care.

YOUNG FAMILIES
In the case of young families, it is often the children who are the motivating force in deciding to get a Cocker puppy. If Mum or

Dad is at home for most of the day with the children, there may not be the same worries about providing care for a pup. But careful consideration must still be given as to whether the whole family is committed to getting a dog. The parent at home is the one who will be responsible for the day-to-day care and training of the pup, so he or she must be just as enthusiastic about getting a Cocker as the children!

It is important to remember that looking after a puppy is very demanding and time-consuming. If you have very young children, do you have the time and energy needed to devote to training and cleaning up after a puppy? Of course, a Cocker puppy is a delight but never underestimate the sheer hard work involved in caring for a pup (something that often comes as a surprise to many a new owner). Also remember that as your puppy grows, his exercise and grooming needs will increase accordingly. These tasks will have to be fitted into the day, no matter how busy you might be with other family responsibilities.

A SUITABLE HOME?

A Cocker's compact size and adaptable nature means he can be just as happy in a small house in the city as in a big home in the country (provided his exercise needs are met). While the size of the garden is not all that important, it is essential that it is fully secure. This means that there must be a good-sized fence or wall (minimum of 5 ft/1.5 m) that must be in good repair. A Cocker puppy can squeeze through very small holes and is also capable of digging under fences. Attention must also be paid to security, ensuring that gates can be locked, as, sadly, the theft of pedigree dogs from gardens is not unknown.

A house with a secure garden is the ideal but a Cocker can adapt to living in an apartment, as long as the owner can provide adequate exercise facilities. If you live in a flat and are thinking of buying a Cocker puppy, you need to be aware that house training

Cockers enjoy the outdoors life, but they can also adapt to being apartment dwellers.

will inevitably take much longer and will involve considerably more effort if you do not have access to your own private garden. You also need to be aware that your neighbours in the flats above or below may not appreciate the noise of a dog crying or barking. If this is likely to be a problem, it may not be the right time to share your life with a Cocker.

You will have double the fun if you take your Cocker on holiday.

HOLIDAY PLANS

Once you own a Cocker Spaniel, you will no longer have the freedom to take off for a day out or weekend away on impulse, as arrangements for your dog must always be considered first. Holidays must be planned with your Cocker's needs in mind as well as your own. Many families enjoy taking their dog away with them on holiday, and there are many holiday cottages, hotels and campsites that accept well-behaved pets. Since the introduction of the Pet Passport scheme, it is also now possible to take your Cocker on holiday outside the UK, provided the destination is included in the scheme and your dog has received all the necessary veterinary treatment necessary.

However, if you are unable to take your Cocker on holiday, you will need to use boarding facilities. Licensed boarding kennels are widely advertised, but it is best to find one via personal recommendation where possible. It is always advisable to visit potential kennels before making a booking to decide whether you are happy with the standard of care and the facilities on offer. Alternatives to boarding kennels include using a home-sitting agency, where sitters come to your home to look after your house and pets, or home boarding, where someone boards your pet in their own home. If you are interested in either of these two options, it is essential to check references and ensure individuals are insured and licensed (in the case of home boarders). Also, bear in mind that the costs of boarding your Cocker while you are away can considerably add to the cost of a family holiday.

WHAT DO YOU WANT FROM YOUR COCKER?

The Cocker Spaniel has long been divided into two distinct types: the show-type Cocker and the working-type Cocker. Many would-be owners of a Cocker

Cocker Spaniels bred from show lines make wonderful companion dogs.

Spaniel are unaware of this distinction, which can lead to confusion and the possibility of a puppy being purchased for a lifestyle to which it is unsuited. The section below aims to describe the main differences between the two Cocker types, to help you make an informed decision about which type would suit your lifestyle best.

Most people's idea of a Cocker Spaniel is epitomised by the show Cocker, with the typical domed head, low-set ears, compact body and glamorous long coat (which inevitably involves time spent on regular grooming and trimming). The show-type Cocker, as the name suggests, is bred for exhibition in the show ring and therefore

resembles the Breed Standard as closely as possible. However, it should be stressed that a show-type Cocker does not have to be shown and, indeed, most live as family pets. Photos of this type of Cocker are often used to illustrate calendars, magazine articles and books about the breed. Although most show-type dogs no longer fulfil the original function of the breed (as a working gundog), many are still capable of doing this job, although their hunting instincts may not be so highly developed as their working cousins.

The working Cocker is bred to perform the function of a working gundog and, as such, physical appearance as laid down by the Breed Standard is not

considered as important as working ability. As we have discovered, the working Cocker is a rangier-looking dog and lacks the glamorous feathering of the show-type. A working Cocker can make a good family pet for the active home, but would-be owners need to be aware that they are taking on an intelligent, high-energy dog with a strong working drive. Such dogs need mental stimulation as well as physical exercise to keep their brains occupied and prevent boredom. For this reason, pet working Cockers are often trained for activities such as agility, flyball and competitive obedience (if owners are not interested in training their dog to the gun).

A Cocker bred from working lines will need extra stimulation, such as competing in agility if it is not being used as a gundog.

Potential owners need to think carefully about what kind of home they can offer, and what activities they are interested in pursuing with their Cocker. If you want a Cocker as a shooting companion, then a working Cocker would be the obvious choice (although show-type Cockers can and do work). If, on the other hand, you are interested in showing your Cocker, then a show-type dog from a reputable show breeder is really the only choice. If you are interested in a Cocker as a pet, either type could suit you, depending on your level of dog training experience and the time you have available for exercise and involvement in canine activities. If you are a first-time dog owner, then you may be wiser to choose a show-type Cocker, whereas if you lead an active, outdoor life and have dog training experience and an interest in activities like agility, then you might prefer a working dog.

FINDING A BREEDER

It can be very difficult for people looking to buy a Cocker puppy to know where to find a reputable breeder. Cockers are hugely popular, which has meant there are many breeders who produce puppies purely for financial gain; they have little interest in the health and temperament of their puppies and will not be willing or able to provide any after-sales help or advice. Distinguishing this type of breeder from the responsible breeder who does everything possible to breed happy, healthy puppies, is not always easy, so you need to do your homework first and be prepared to ask as many questions as possible. Here are examples of questions you should ask a breeder:

DO YOU SHOW OR WORK YOUR DOGS?
Reputable breeders will often have a longstanding, serious interest in Cocker Spaniels – they will take part in activities with their dogs, such as showing, field work (in the case of working Cockers), agility, or obedience training. This type of breeder will be a member of a least one breed club, such as The Cocker Spaniel Club (the parent club for Cocker Spaniels), as well as other regional breed clubs. Be wary of breeders whose only interest in Cocker Spaniels is in the

MALE OR FEMALE?

For many, the choice between a dog and a bitch comes down to personal preference. There is not a vast difference in size or temperament between the sexes, as there are in some breeds, and both male and female Cockers make equally good companions. It is important to remember that every Cocker is an individual, so it is simply not possible to make generalisations such as "bitches are easier to train than dogs" or "dogs are more loyal and affectionate than bitches". Some bitches may well be easier than some dogs, but the reverse can also be true!

If a bitch is chosen, then consideration must be given to the fact that she will come into season when mature, and, during a season, she must be kept away from entire males, which may restrict exercise opportunities. Seasons will continue approximately every six to nine months unless the decision is made to neuter at the appropriate time.

It is true that an entire male can become very distracted by the scent of a bitch in season, but unless you live close to an entire bitch, or exercise your dog where bitches in season are also regularly exercised, an entire male Cocker is not generally any less reliable off lead than a Cocker bitch, provided he is well trained. Such concerns can be alleviated by neutering your male Cocker.

Cockers are very much individuals – but both male and female make equally good companions.

breeding and sale of puppies, as those who breed purely for profit do not have the breed's best interests at heart.

WHAT HEALTH-SCREENING TESTS DO YOU CARRY OUT ON YOUR DOGS?

As with most pedigree dogs, a number of hereditary conditions are occasionally seen in the breed, but good breeders will test their breeding animals to ensure their puppies are as healthy as possible. Such tests include:

- Annual eye tests. A number of eye conditions are seen in the Cocker Spaniel, but there are two known to be hereditary and that result in blindness: GPRA (general progressive retinal atrophy) and CPRA (central progressive retinal atrophy). Glaucoma is also known to exist in the breed. There is a one-off test for predisposition to glaucoma (goniodysgenesis) and an annual eye test for the two other conditions.
- DNA tests exist for prcd-PRA (also known as GPRA as above) and FN (familial nephropathy, a fatal kidney disease that affects young Cockers). These new gene tests enable breeders to avoid breeding puppies affected with either of these two conditions since carriers can now be identified before being bred from.
- Hip scoring. There is evidence of hip dysplasia in some Cocker Spaniels, and breeders are now beginning to score their dogs to evaluate how serious this problem is.

Remember that if puppies are described as 'vet checked', this does not mean their parents have had the tests described above. Check if the parents have been tested for the above conditions and ask to see the relevant certificates. (For more information on inherited conditions, see Chapter Eight.)

CAN I MEET THE PUPPIES' MOTHER?

A good breeder will always encourage would-be buyers to meet the mother of a litter, plus other close relatives that live with the breeder. This is a good chance to check that the breeder's dogs all have happy, outgoing temperaments. Puppy farmers and dealers (who buy puppies to sell on) will often tell buyers that the mother is "at the vet" or "away on holiday". Never be tempted to accept such excuses; you should always insist on being able to see the mother, and if you can't, walk away. When you do meet the mother, be wary if she seems nervous or distressed – unless her puppies are very

You will want to see the mother with her puppies, as this will give you a good idea of the temperament they are likely to inherit.

young. Most Cocker mothers are happy to meet visitors and will let them handle the puppies.

Since good breeders will often travel miles to use the most suitable stud dog for their litters, it is unlikely that the sire of the litter will be available for viewing. However, the breeder should be happy to show you photos of him and give you contact details for the stud dog owner should you be interested in arranging a visit.

ARE PUPPIES REARED IN THE HOME?

Puppies who have been born and reared inside the breeder's home are often at an advantage to those reared outside in kennels since they will be used to the sights and sounds of a normal household, such as the noise of the telephone and vacuum cleaner. They will also be used to people coming and going and will probably have received more individual handling by family members than those reared outside. However if puppies are kennel reared, do make sure they are being kept in a clean, warm environment with plenty of toys for stimulation, and that the pups are used to being handled by a variety of people. Do not be tempted to buy a puppy kept in dirty, badly maintained kennels or in over-crowded conditions with lots of other puppies.

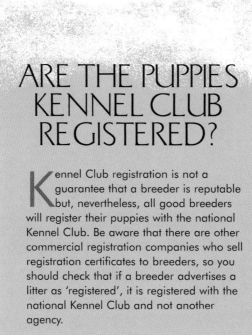

ARE THE PUPPIES KENNEL CLUB REGISTERED?

Kennel Club registration is not a guarantee that a breeder is reputable but, nevertheless, all good breeders will register their puppies with the national Kennel Club. Be aware that there are other commercial registration companies who sell registration certificates to breeders, so you should check that if a breeder advertises a litter as 'registered', it is registered with the national Kennel Club and not another agency.

WHAT COLOURS ARE AVAILABLE?

Cocker Spaniels come in numerous attractive colours, but some colours are more widely available than others. It is therefore best not to set your heart on a particular colour (particularly the rarer colours) unless you are prepared to be extremely patient. Unfortunately, less reputable breeders will often 'specialise' in producing whichever colours are currently in demand with the general public, but remember that temperament and health are far more important than colour. You will find it easier to find a suitable litter from a reputable breeder if you can be flexible about the colour you want.

ARE ANY PUPPIES BOOKED ALREADY?

Breeders with good reputations often do not need to advertise their litters, so don't be surprised if you contact a breeder and some puppies are already pre-booked. Good breeders may have a waiting list for their puppies, so you cannot necessarily expect to have 'first' or even 'second choice' of any litter, unless you have contacted a breeder well in advance. Breeders will often want to keep a puppy for themselves and will allow the buyers to choose after they have made their own selection. Sometimes this means that you may only have a choice between a few puppies rather than the whole litter, but this can make the decision-making process easier since most puppy buyers find it very hard to pick one puppy out from a litter of six or seven equally lovely puppies.

ARE THE PUPPIES WORMED AND VACCINATED?

All puppies should be wormed every two weeks from two to three weeks of age. Make sure the breeder can tell you about their worming programme and ask about the specific treatment used.

Most Cocker puppies will leave for their new homes at eight weeks of age. Breeders will not generally vaccinate before this age because young puppies have immunity from their mother for

In most cases, puppies will not be vaccinated before they leave the breeder's home.

some time, meaning that vaccination too early will be ineffective. Your vet will advise on the recommended vaccination protocols once you have brought your puppy home.

HOW DO I FIND A REPUTABLE BREEDER?

The Cocker Spaniel breed clubs offer excellent resources of information to help you begin your search. The secretaries of each club should be able to recommend breeders who have puppies available or planned. Contact details for all the breed clubs can be found by getting in touch with the Kennel Club in the UK or the American Kennel Club (see Appendices). The Kennel Club operates a Puppy Sales Register, which can be accessed via the KC website, and a similar Puppy Referral Service is offered by the AKC. It is best to avoid classified adverts and free ad publications/websites, as these are frequently used by puppy farmers and dealers who can be extremely clever at portraying themselves as genuine, caring breeders when this is far from the truth. While some good breeders do use these sources to advertise, they are in the minority, so please be careful and never accept any advert at face value without doing further research.

VIEWING THE PUPPIES

If you are looking for a puppy for a specific purpose, such as showing or working, then it is vital that the breeders you visit are experienced and successful in those fields. As a new puppy buyer, you will be relying on the experience of the breeder to guide you towards the most suitable puppy for your needs. No breeder can ever guarantee that a puppy will be a Crufts winner or a good working dog, but they will use their experience and knowledge to pick out those puppies with the most potential.

If you are choosing a puppy for a companion only, an experienced breeder can give

GENERAL GUIDELINES TO FOLLOW

- Remember that price is not everything. Puppies are not like household commodities where you can shop around for the best deal. Reputable breeders do not sell their puppies cheaply, and while it might be tempting to respond to an advert offering puppies at less than the going rate, the puppy may not be such a bargain in the long run. On the other hand, a high asking price is not necessarily a guarantee of quality either.

- Expect to be vetted. Reputable breeders will want to find out as much about you and your home as possible, so do not be offended if you are asked a series of questions about your house and garden, your work situation, and how old your children are (if any). These questions show that the breeder genuinely cares about his/her puppies and wants to find the best possible homes for them. Be wary of any breeder who asks no questions at all – such breeders care little for their puppies and are only interested in making a quick sale.

- Be patient. Reputable breeders do not have a constant supply of puppies, and it may be the case that potential buyers will have to wait weeks, perhaps even months, for a suitable litter to be born. Mistakes are often made by buyers who will not wait – they want a puppy now – and so they rush out and buy in haste (perhaps ignoring the warning signs that the breeder is not reputable). Remember, with any luck you will have your Cocker for 10 to 15 years – what is a wait of a few months for the 'right' puppy compared to this?

- Never buy a puppy because you feel sorry for it, either because it appears shy or fearful, or because you are unhappy with the conditions in which it is being reared. This is a recipe for disaster, as you could end up with a puppy that has severe health and temperament problems (and you will be helping less reputable breeders to stay in business).

Make sure you buy the right puppy by following some basic guidelines.

All puppies are irresistible, so it is best to seek the breeder's advice to help you choose the puppy most suited to your lifestyle.

guidance as to a puppy's likely temperament by indicating to visitors which pup is the most confident, and which may be a little sensitive. This will help you to choose the pup with the most suitable temperament for your particular home. For example, if you have no previous dog experience, it may be wise to avoid the most confident puppy in the litter (since this pup may prove too challenging for novice owners), and instead choose a more laidback puppy. However, you should avoid any litter where puppies cower away from visitors or attempt to hide in a corner, as this suggests nervousness and timidity.

After satisfying yourself that all puppies in the litter are happy to be handled by visitors, you should also check that their eyes are bright with no signs of discharge, and their ears are clean and sweet smelling. Make sure their coats are also clean with no dry, flaky skin. Cocker puppies should also be sturdy and have nicely rounded bodies, being neither too thin (which could indicate poor nutrition) or pot-bellied (which could indicate a worm burden).

A SHOW PUPPY
If you are looking for a potential show puppy, the breeder will select the pup that most closely resembles the Breed Standard, in miniature, by assessing the puppy's physical conformation. The breeder will also evaluate temperament. A show prospect should be outgoing, with a certain 'look at me' quality. The puppy should have the correct scissor bite (although bites can change as a puppy grows), and, if the pup is a male, he should have two descended testicles.

A WORKING PUPPY
If you are hoping for a potential working dog, you should look for a puppy whose parents have proven working ability, and the pedigree to match. You will be looking for FT. Ch./Field Trial Champions in the pedigree rather than Sh. Ch./Show Champions. Physical appearance will not be as relevant as for a show puppy, but you will still be looking for a correct bite and good, balanced conformation. Temperament is also important. A sensitive puppy may not be able to cope with the

When puppies are small, it is hard to distinguish between puppies bred from show lines (left) and puppies from working lines (right).

demands of training for the field, but an overly bold puppy may be too hard to train for a novice. The breeder should be able to tell you about the individual personalities of the puppies to help you make your choice.

CHOOSING AN ADULT/RESCUED COCKER

Sometimes people prefer to rehome an older rescue dog rather than a demanding puppy. However, an older Cocker should not necessarily be seen as the 'easy' option since rescued dogs may need special care and training, depending on their backgrounds. Some will have been ill-treated in their former homes and will need understanding new owners who can work on their rehabilitation.

Others may have been loved in their previous homes but may not have received adequate training, meaning there could be behavioural problems that a new owner will need to address. Of course, not all rescue Cockers have problems, but even those with no known issues will need time and patience to settle into new homes. New owners need to understand that there may be initial lapses in house training, for example.

There are many sources of rescued Cockers, from big, well-funded national centres to small independent rescues. A good rescue organisation will try to assess all dogs prior to offering them for rehoming, and will also offer back-up help and advice once a dog goes to a new home.

Potential owners will be screened for suitability, which often involves a home-check carried out by a volunteer to ensure that the home in question is right for the dog that has been chosen. Ideally, rescued dogs should be neutered prior to rehoming, and examined by a vet to make sure there are no ongoing health problems that will need treatment.

If you are interested in a rescued Cocker, you should find out as much as you can about the dog's background. If you are out at work for part of the day, you need to check that the rescued dog does not suffer from separation anxiety and can safely be left alone for reasonable periods. If you have cats, you need to be sure that the rescued

If you are thinking about taking on a rescued Cocker, try to find out as much about the dog's background as possible.

dog is 'cat friendly'. Similarly, if you have another dog, you need to establish whether the rescued dog gets on well with other dogs.

If you have young children, it would be very risky to take on an older dog without a known history. Dogs who are not used to children or are afraid of them may sometimes react aggressively with tragic consequences. For this reason, it is important that you only consider dogs assessed as suitable for living with children. However, you should be aware that many reputable rescues would not let a rescued dog go to a home where there are young children under a certain age. This policy exists because it can be very difficult to assess how an older dog will react to living with very small children, particularly if that dog has not lived with children before.

OTHER SOURCES OF OLDER DOGS

Older Cockers are sometimes advertised for sale by their existing owners. Sometimes, there is a genuine reason for an owner wanting to sell their Cocker, but equally there may be problems with behaviour or health, which you may not find out about until it is too late. For this reason, private sale adverts should always be viewed with caution. If you have children, you should be particularly cautious, as dogs may be advertised as being 'good with children' when this may not be the case.

Breeders may also occasionally have older Cockers available for rehoming or sale. If such a dog has been kept outside in kennels with little socialisation, he may have difficulty adjusting to family life and may react badly to being kept as an only dog if he is used to the company of other dogs. However, if the breeder can show you that the dog is well socialised and well trained, there should be few problems adjusting to a new home. However, do make sure that the breeder is willing to take the dog back if you find that he does not settle well with you (after allowing a reasonable time for this to happen).

SUMMARY

If you follow the guidance in this chapter, taking your time and doing as much research as possible before committing yourself to a Cocker Spaniel, you will find that your time has been well spent, and you will be rewarded with the joys of sharing your home with a happy, healthy Cocker for many years to come.

If you choose the Cocker Spaniel to suit your lifestyle, you can look forward to many years of happy companionship.

THE NEW ARRIVAL

Once you have found your new Cocker puppy or rescued Cocker, you should begin to prepare for your new arrival, starting with dog-proofing your house and garden.

HOME TASKS

First, you will need to make sure that all electrical cables and wiring are safely secured and inaccessible to an inquisitive puppy; puppies and young dogs will pull and chew at loose, hanging cables with possibly disastrous results. Remove indoor plants and put them out of harm's way, as a puppy will be tempted to chew any foliage within reach (and eat the compost too sometimes!). Then make sure that potentially dangerous household chemicals and medicines are also safely out of reach in a locked cupboard.

If you are buying a puppy, a sensible purchase would be a stairgate to close off the stairs, as allowing puppies to run up and down stairs can damage growth plates and put a strain on immature joints. If your house is a modern, open-plan design, you may also want to consider using a stairgate to keep your new addition confined to a safe area (e.g. a kitchen or utility room) for the times when you cannot supervise him.

GARDEN CHECKS

Your garden needs to be totally secure, so check that your fencing is in good order with no holes for a Cocker to escape through. If you have a pond, make sure it is covered or temporarily blocked

A Cocker puppy can get up to all sorts of mischief, so make sure your garden is safe and secure.

off so the puppy cannot accidentally fall in. Young puppies have been known to drown in garden ponds. You will need to protect any precious plants or shrubs, as Cockers like to dig holes and chew plants and cannot distinguish between a prized floral specimen and a weed! Beware of any poisonous plants in your garden, which a puppy (or older dog) might be tempted to chew and eat. Common garden plants that are poisonous to dogs include: foxgloves, laburnum, rhubarb, sweet peas, chrysanthemums, and daffodil and tulip bulbs. As with household chemicals, make sure all garden chemicals and pesticides are safely locked away at all times.

If you have a large garden and are bringing a Cocker puppy into your home, you might want to consider temporarily enclosing a smaller area for a puppy to use. This will help with house training, as puppies are often distracted if they have a very large area in which to explore and play.

BUYING EQUIPMENT

Whether your new arrival is a puppy or an older Cocker, you will need to invest in various items of essential equipment to help your dog settle in his new home.

CRATE/PLAY PEN

If you are buying a puppy, a playpen or a crate will provide your pup with a safe, secure area to call his own. A playpen usually consists of a number of metal panels, which clip together to form an enclosed area, where you will put your pup's bed and toys. Your pup then has a place to sleep and room to play when you are not able to supervise him.

However, a puppy pen does take up considerable space, so if you have a small house, this may not be a viable option. An alternative would be a crate that should be big enough for an adult Cocker to stand up comfortably and lie down in fully stretched out - 24 in x 18 in x 21 in high (61 cm x 45 cm x 53 cm) is the minimum recommended size for a Cocker. A crate provides a safe haven for a pup or adult dog to be left in for short periods, or to sleep in at night, and can aid house training since puppies do not usually like to soil their bed areas.

There are many crates available on the market; some are made from wire mesh and some from plastic or fabric. A wire mesh crate is best for a young puppy since it cannot be chewed or ripped. Crates are also useful for an older, rescued dog, who will often appreciate having a cosy space to call his own, although care must be taken to introduce crates slowly to puppies/dogs who are not used to them (see page 58). If you are investing in a crate, several pieces of polyester fleece-type bedding are ideal for a puppy, as they wash and dry easily and are more resistant to being chewed. Older dogs may prefer a soft duvet-style bed for their crate.

A Cocker will soon learn to see his crate as a special doggy den.

TOYS

There is a huge range of dog toys available. If you are buying a puppy, you need to ensure that the toys you buy are safe for puppies and are not small enough to be swallowed or too easily chewed up. Safe chew toys for Cocker puppies and adults include nylon bones and large rawhide chews (smaller rawhide chews should be avoided, as they are too easily swallowed whole). There are also special puppy chew toys available, which can be frozen to help a pup with sore gums at the teething stage. Squeaky toys and soft toys are also popular with Cockers, but they need to be used under close supervision so they can be removed immediately at the first sign of disintegration!

Activity toys are also popular. These toys are designed to entertain dogs and keep them occupied in their owner's absence; they usually involve food or treats being stuffed into the toy, which the dog has to work at to release. Examples include the popular rubber Kongs, which come in various sizes and can be stuffed with food or thrown, and also treat balls/cubes.

Play toys range from the cheap and cheerful, such as balls and Frisbees, to the more expensive options, such as bubble machines with meat-flavoured bubbles! Cockers love to retrieve balls and other toys designed for throwing, but never give your Cocker a ball that is small enough to be swallowed. Also remember: never play with or throw a stick; sticks can cause horrendous injuries and even death if they get lodged in a dog's mouth.

DOG BED

If you are investing in a crate, it is best to use this as your Cocker's only bed with the bedding recommended above. If you prefer not to use a crate, or are using a playpen instead, your next purchase should be a bed for your new addition. If you are buying a puppy, a plastic bed is easier to clean and more chew-resistant. It can be lined with a piece of polyester bedding as recommended above. Older Cockers may prefer one of the softly padded fabric beds or beanbags now widely available, but these are best avoided for puppies or young dogs still at the chewing stage. Old-fashioned wicker baskets may look attractive but they are easily chewed and very difficult to clean.

There is a huge variety of toys to choose from – make sure the toys you buy are safe for your Cocker.

OTHER EQUIPMENT

Other essential items include a food and water bowl. Ceramic or stainless steel bowls are popular and are widely available in the normal dog-bowl shape. Alternatively, there are Spaniel bowls, which have high tapered sides specially designed to let a Cocker's ears drop either side of the bowl so they don't get covered in food. Spaniel bowls are not essential for a puppy whose ears are relatively short, but are highly recommended for adult Cockers.

Collars and leads come in a variety of materials and colours, and personal preference will largely dictate which type you go for. For a puppy, it is best to start with a lightweight nylon collar and lead, which will be strong and chew-resistant but not too heavy for a pup. For adult Cockers, some owners prefer a rolled leather collar, as opposed to the traditional flat collar, as this leaves less of a mark on a Cocker's fine, silky coat. Harnesses and head collars may also be used when training a puppy or adult dog to walk on the lead, but these are not essential first purchases. Please don't be tempted to buy an old-fashioned choke chain collar for a Cocker Spaniel; such collars are easily misused and can cause injury as a result.

FINDING A VET

Before your Cocker arrives, it makes sense to register with a vet in advance so you can get advice on subjects such as vaccinations and neutering beforehand, and also check that you are happy with the services offered before you ever need to use them. Recommendations from family, friends or neighbours are often the best way to find a good vet in your area. Alternatively, you could visit several local practices and choose one based on factors such as the friendliness of the staff and the range of services on offer. Once you have chosen a vet, make an appointment for your pup or rescued dog to have a basic check up a few days after coming home to you. This will enable you to chat to the vet about vaccination protocols and worming programmes, and give you peace of mind that your new arrival is in good health.

Finally, you will need to purchase a basic grooming kit so you can get your new Cocker used to being groomed as soon as possible. For puppies, your starter kit should include a small bristle brush, a soft slicker brush and a comb. For adults, your basic items will include a larger slicker brush, a fine-toothed comb, a wide-toothed comb and possibly scissors and nail clippers. You can add to your grooming equipment later, depending on whether you intend trimming your Cocker yourself or using the services of a professional groomer (see Chapter Five).

IDENTIFICATION

Identification is a very important part of responsible pet ownership, as, sadly, it is not uncommon for dogs to go missing. The most popular method of permanent identification of dogs is the insertion of a tiny microchip underneath the skin. This microchip contains details of a dog's owners and their address, which are recorded on a national database and can be used to reunite or identify a dog if it ever goes missing.

Another method of identification is tattooing, whereby a unique number is tattooed inside a dog's ear (or sometimes inside the thigh). The dog's ownership details are then logged on to a national database, as with microchipping.

Some breeders and many rescue centres will microchip their dogs before they go to new homes, so new owners simply have to change the contact details recorded on the national database. If your puppy or rescued dog does not come into this category, you can easily arrange for microchipping to be carried out by your vet.

Even if your Cocker is permanently identified by microchip or tattoo, it is a legal requirement for your name and address (not just your telephone number) to be recorded on an identity tag attached to the collar.

COLLECTING YOUR COCKER

In the excitement of collecting your Cocker puppy, paperwork may seem unimportant but you should check that you receive all the necessary documentation from your breeder. You should expect to receive a copy of your pup's pedigree (four- or five-generation) and Kennel Club registration documents. If this is not available for any reason, you should ensure the breeder gives you a written promise that the registration papers will follow. You may also be asked to sign a puppy sales contract by the breeder. Read this through carefully and ask the breeder to explain anything you don't understand. Puppy contracts are often used by responsible breeders to let you know formally about any endorsements that may be placed on your pup's registration, and to cover conditions such as a buyer agreeing to return a puppy to the breeder if it ever needs rehoming.

As well as formal documentation, you should be given a detailed diet sheet, information about worming protocols, guidance on training and grooming, and a vaccination booklet (if the breeder has already started the vaccination programme). Good breeders will also often supply toys and a blanket/bedding, which smells of your pup's littermates, to help him settle in more easily to your home. It is also common practice for breeders to supply a small bag of the food that your pup is used to eating. You should keep your pup on this food for at least a week or two to give him time to

At last the day comes when it is time to collect your puppy.

settle in. Do not be tempted suddenly to offer a different food because your puppy seems picky or not hungry when he arrives home with you. It is very common for puppies to lose their appetite somewhat when they leave the breeder due to the excitement of new people and a new home, but they soon get back to normal if you give them enough time. However, if you constantly chop and change the food, you will end up with a faddy eater who knows that if he turns his nose up at one meal, you will offer him something different the next time!

MEETING THE FAMILY

Once you have collected your Cocker puppy or rescued dog, it is time to introduce him to your family and your other pets (if any). The following advice refers mainly to introducing a new puppy, but is also relevant to those introducing an adult dog to their home.

CHILDREN

Your children will naturally be very excited when you bring your new Cocker home, but try to keep the introductions as calm and quiet as possible. If you have bought a puppy, remember that it

MEETING THE FAMILY

Cockers and children can be a great combination, but early interactions should be supervised.

Cockers are very collectable, and as long as you are tactful, the resident dog will soon accept the newcomer.

is a big upheaval in his life to leave his littermates behind and to move to a totally new home, so try not to over-face him with too much noise and excitement at first. Young children often want to hug and cuddle a dog, but this can be overwhelming to a new arrival, so encourage your children to be gentle and show them where a dog often likes to be stroked (under the chin or on the chest is better than a pat on the head, which many dogs find uncomfortable).

Children can be allowed to hold a puppy while they are sitting down, but don't let them pick up a pup and carry him around, as it is easy for a wriggly puppy to jump out of a child's arms and fall to the ground, resulting in possibly serious

injury. Teach your children the right way to hold your puppy, which means supporting him under the chest and under the bottom (not holding him by the chest and letting the back legs dangle free). Remember that moving to a new home is tiring and initially stressful for every puppy or adult dog, so make sure your children give your new arrival space and time to rest when he needs it.

OTHER DOGS

It is generally a good idea to introduce a new dog to an existing family dog on neutral territory (i.e. not inside your home), and then bring the new arrival and resident dog into the house together. This may not be possible with a young,

unvaccinated puppy, so some owners have found that leaving a new puppy in the garden and then letting the resident dog go to find the new arrival is a method that works very successfully, under careful owner supervision, of course.

When introducing a new puppy or older dog to an existing dog, you need to be patient and allow plenty of time for the new arrival to be accepted. However, it can take weeks, if not longer, for a resident dog to fully accept a new canine arrival, so try not to panic if your existing dog seems resentful of your new Cocker. This is not uncommon and does not mean that that the two will not eventually become the best of friends.

CATS

Puppies will generally learn to live happily with feline company; they are small enough not to be able to inflict damage on a cat, which will inevitably be much quicker on its feet than any Cocker puppy. You will need to supervise first encounters, as a small puppy is more at risk of injury from an adult cat than vice versa. Make sure your cat has a safe haven to retreat to, which is not accessible to your puppy, e.g. install a stairgate so your cat can go upstairs without the pup following. If your cat is very timid, keep him/her inside the house for a few weeks, otherwise the shock of the new arrival could cause a reluctance to come home at all. Make sure you feed your cats where your pup cannot get their food – puppies often find cat food more appealing than their own food! Finally, remember to put your cat's litter tray somewhere inaccessible to your pup; puppies and some older dogs will often eat cat faeces when given the opportunity to do so.

If your new arrival is an older rescued Cocker, you need to be aware that dogs not brought up with cats may be hostile towards them, which could inevitably be dangerous for any resident cat. Even if your rescued Cocker has been assessed as cat-friendly, you should still carefully supervise first encounters and follow the above advice in relation to puppies.

Remember, a puppy is much more vulnerable than a cat when they first meet.

Make sure that your existing dog has a place of his own to escape to for some peace and quiet (puppies can be particularly exhausting for older dogs) and never leave new and existing dogs together unsupervised for at least the first few weeks. A puppy pen or crate will be very useful if you are introducing a puppy to a home with an existing dog, as you will have a secure place to leave your pup when you have to go out or when your existing dog needs some quiet time away from a lively pup.

OTHER PETS

It has been known for a Cocker puppy to happily share his home with a house rabbit as long as ground rules are laid down from the start, such as never allowing a puppy to chase the rabbit and making sure all encounters are closely supervised. Introductions need to be made slowly and calmly and, initially, your puppy should be on a lead so that he cannot chase or charge the rabbit. Never leave your puppy and rabbit alone together (use a playpen or crate for the times you cannot supervise your puppy). Other small pets, such as hamsters, guinea pigs and gerbils, should always be safely secured inside their own housing/hutches when your puppy is out and about. If you do allow such pets to have free-running time in your house, make sure your puppy is safely inside his crate or playpen.

NB: If you are introducing an older rescued Cocker, you should be aware that dogs not brought up with other pets may have a strong instinct to hunt/chase small animals, meaning they can never be trusted with small furries, including house rabbits.

CRATE TRAINING

As mentioned earlier, a crate can be extremely useful as a safe, secure place for your puppy to sleep in, or to use when you have to go out for short periods. The important thing to remember is that crate training must be a slow, gradual process. You should never buy a crate and shut your puppy inside without first getting him used to the idea.

Make the crate as cosy and comfortable as possible with soft bedding and some toys, and encourage your pup to go in the crate with the door open by throwing treats inside. Then feed your pup his meals inside the crate, so he begins to associate it with positive experiences (i.e. food and treats). Once your pup is happy to go in and out of the crate and to take naps inside with the door open, you can start to close the door for short periods (perhaps

Take time introducing your puppy to his crate.

only a minute or two to begin with), gradually building up to longer periods.

It can help to cover the crate with a blanket or towel, as this makes it even cosier for your pup, but ensure there is still plenty of ventilation. If you are using a crate to help with house training a pup and have bought a crate big enough for an adult Cocker, you may find that you need to make the crate interior smaller, as if there is too much room, your pup may use his crate to toilet in. You can make the crate smaller by blocking off a section (you can now buy readymade partitions for this purpose).

Some pups will cry when they realise they cannot get out of the crate, but this is less likely to happen if you have spent time (perhaps as long as a week or two) getting your puppy used to his crate with the door open. If your pup does whine, wait for him to stop (even if this only lasts a few seconds) before letting him out. You don't want your puppy to learn that if he makes a noise, you will immediately open the crate door! Never shut your puppy in the crate as a punishment for unwanted behaviour; you want your puppy to see his crate as his own safe little haven, not somewhere where unpleasant things happen. Also never use a crate to contain a puppy for hours on end (apart from at night). A crate should be used for short periods of time only, no longer than two hours during the day for a young puppy or a little longer for a mature, adult dog.

Adult dogs can be crate trained in just the same way as described

A puppy will feel bewildered when he first arrives in his new home.

for a puppy, but you may need to be patient, as it can take considerably longer to crate train an older dog.

THE FIRST NIGHT

There are various approaches to settling your new puppy for his first night in your home. The old-fashioned method is to choose where your puppy will sleep at night (often a bed or crate in the kitchen or utility room), then just leave him to it, ignoring all crying

and howling. There is no doubt that this method will work if persevered with, since a puppy will eventually cease to cry/howl if there is never a reaction. However, it seems very harsh when you take into account that this is a young animal taken away from everything and everyone he has ever known, who is suddenly thrust into a totally new environment. It also ignores the need for a young puppy to toilet during the night (no young puppy will be able to

59

control his bladder or bowels for such a long time).

A kinder method would be to go down to the puppy once or twice during the night to give him the opportunity to go outside and toilet. If you do this, don't make a big fuss of your puppy or play with him – just calmly and quietly take him outside and then put him straight back to bed. Don't go down every time you hear your pup cry, or he will soon learn that he gets your attention whenever he makes a noise. Alternatively, you could have your puppy's bed or crate in the bedroom with you for the first few nights and then gradually move the bed/crate to the area in which you eventually want your puppy to sleep. This method means your puppy will be comforted by your presence during those stressful first nights, and you will hear him easily if he wakes and needs to go outside to toilet.

A piece of familiar bedding or blanket from your pup's breeder will help him settle more easily at night. Your pup will no longer have his littermates to cuddle up with, so a securely covered hot-water bottle may offer him some comfort. You can even buy special puppy heat pads, which come with built-in heartbeat sounds to simulate the sound of a mother's heartbeat.

HOUSE TRAINING

House training a new puppy takes patience and perseverance, and cannot be achieved in a few days or even a few weeks. Young puppies have very little bladder and bowel control, and they also have short attention spans, so new owners have to be prepared for it to sometimes take much longer than they may have expected before their new pup is reliable in the house.

Take your puppy outside at frequent intervals (perhaps every hour to begin with), also after every meal, every time he wakes up after a sleep, and after every energetic play session. At other times, watch out for the signs that your pup needs to go, such as circling round or sniffing the floor intently. Stay outside with your pup until he toilets, encouraging him by repeating a key phrase, such as "Hurry up" or "Be clean". When he does 'go', give him gentle praise (but don't overdo it, as too much excited praise can distract a pup). Eventually your puppy will learn to associate this key phrase with going to the toilet, meaning you will be able to get him to 'go' on command, which can be very useful.

The house training process involves endless repetition and is often frustrating; you may find yourself standing outside in the pouring rain in the middle of your night while your puppy seems far more interested in chasing a leaf than going to the toilet! However, if you persevere, your puppy will eventually get the message and

Be patient when you take your puppy out into the garden for toileting purposes, and reward him with lots of praise when he responds correctly.

HOUSE RULES

When introducing your new Cocker to your home, it is important that all members of the family understand the house rules and apply them consistently. For example, if you have decided that you do not want your Cocker to sit on the sofa or other furniture, every family member must stick to this rule. A dog will get very confused if some of the family allows him to share the sofa and some don't! Don't encourage your puppy in any behaviour that you would not tolerate in an adult. For example, it may be amusing when a puppy nibbles on Dad's favourite slippers, but it won't be so funny when that puppy is old enough to totally destroy them. Similarly, children need to be taught to pick up their clothing and toys and not leave them lying around; a puppy cannot be expected to distinguish between his own toys (allowed) and the children's toys (not allowed).

If you have a young family, the following house rules are essential for the safety of both dog and children:

• Never leave any puppy or adult dog alone unsupervised with young children. This is particularly important if you are introducing a rescued dog, even one who has been previously assessed as suitable for living with children.
• Never wake up a sleeping puppy or dog.
• Never tease, poke or prod a puppy or dog.

accidents inside the house will gradually decrease as the weeks go by.

Some owners prefer to start training a puppy to toilet on newspaper or special puppy pads inside the house. However, this could confuse a puppy and make house training take longer since you are in effect training a puppy that it is acceptable to toilet in the house (even if it is on paper/pads). Never punish your puppy for having an accident in the house – puppies do not understand human concepts of right and wrong, and will not even remember having the accident if it happened more than a few seconds ago. If you catch your puppy in the act, say "No" firmly and then take him outside as quickly as possible. If you do find a puddle, just calmly clear it up and resolve to keep a closer eye on your puppy in future. Incidentally, puppy accidents are best cleaned up with biological soap powder, not household disinfectants (which often contain ingredients that smell like urine to a puppy, so attracting him back to the same spot).

The above advice will also be relevant if your new arrival is an older, rescued Cocker, as it is not unusual for some house trained dogs to lapse in their training after being rehomed, probably due to feelings of insecurity and confusion. If this happens, it is best to go back to basics and treat your rescued Cocker exactly like a puppy until he gets the hang of things again. Don't be surprised or annoyed if you do come across an occasional accident, and never punish a rescued dog for making a mistake inside your home; you need to gain his trust and confidence. This advice is especially important if your rescued dog has had a long period of being kennelled outside, or has never known of a life inside the home with a family, as it can take such dogs a long time to become fully house trained.

FIRST EXPERIENCES

Once your puppy becomes a member of your family, you can start teaching him all the things he will need to learn in order to become a happy, well-adjusted Cocker Spaniel.

A Cocker puppy is very quick to learn, so reward the behaviour you want, and be firm if your pup behaves inappropriately.

brushing and combing your puppy every day for just a few minutes to begin with, using praise and a treat as a reward at the end of every session.

MOUTHING/PUPPY PLAY BITING

Mouthing and play biting are perfectly normal behaviours for a healthy puppy. A puppy who bites and nips is not displaying aggressive tendencies (as some owners think) but simply playing with his human family in the same way he would play with his littermates. Play biting helps a puppy develop good bite inhibition (i.e. not to bite too hard) so is actually a necessary phase of puppy development. With patience and consistency, you can teach your puppy not to bite or mouth tender human skin, but it will take time.

One tactic that can work for some puppies is to yelp loudly (as if in pain) when a puppy bites, which can be enough to interrupt the behaviour. You can then distract the pup by offering one of his own chew toys. However, for some puppies, yelping will just increase their own excitement, causing them to bite even more. For such puppies, the 'time-out' method will probably be more successful. This involves ignoring the puppy for a short time, either by removing yourself from his presence or by placing him in isolation in another room. These time-out sessions need to be short, as a puppy will not be able to remember why he is being ignored if he is left alone for more than a minute or two. All family members also need to stay calm,

HANDLING

From a health point of view, a dog needs to be able to be examined so owners can spot when there may be something wrong. Start by touching your puppy all over his body. Look inside his ears and gently open his mouth, then lift and touch his feet. It helps if you can use a raised surface, such as a table, for this. Keep these practice sessions short with lots of praise and a treat at the end of each 'examination', and soon you will have a puppy that enjoys being

handled and touched. Ask visiting friends or family to do the handling so your puppy gets used to being touched by strangers, too. Visits to the vet will then be made much easier, as your vet will not have to wrestle with a wriggly puppy who hates being handled.

This handling practice can then be extended to grooming sessions. Since regular grooming is very important for a Cocker Spaniel, it is never too early to start teaching a puppy to enjoy being groomed. Use a raised surface, and practise

HANDLING A COCKER PUPPY

If you accustom your puppy to being examined from an early age, it will ensure there are no problems with grooming sessions or visits to the vet when he gets older.

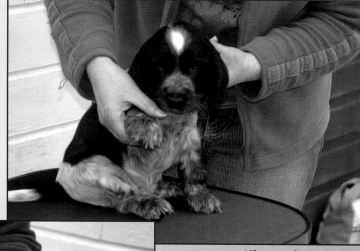

Lift up each paw in turn.

Check the ears.

Open the mouth to inspect teeth and gums.

If you take on an older Cocker, try to establish a regular daily routine, as this will help your dog to settle.

as shouting and shrieking at a puppy will just increase his adrenaline levels, making him bite more. Children should also be taught to sit or stand still 'like a statue' even though their natural tendency is to run and jump about if a puppy is biting their feet! However, a puppy will soon calm down if nobody is reacting to his behaviour.

The key to teaching a puppy not to mouth/play bite is repetition, and a consistent approach from every member of the family. Patience is the order of the day, as with most other aspects of training a new puppy!

COLLAR WEARING

As soon as your puppy arrives home, you can start getting him used to wearing a lightweight puppy collar for short periods. He may well scratch at his neck to begin with, due to the unfamiliar sensation of the collar, but this soon passes, especially if you offer a toy or a game as a distraction.

You may also want to attach a lightweight lead to his collar some of the time so he can get used to this new sensation. Lead walking can then be practised in the garden long before a puppy is old enough to go outside for proper walks.

If you are using a crate to train your puppy, remember to remove his collar before shutting him inside, as, sadly, there have been incidents when collars have become entangled in the wire mesh of a crate with tragic consequences.

SPECIAL CONSIDERATIONS FOR ADULT/RESCUED DOGS

Many new owners of rescued Cockers are anxious to help their new arrival feel at home and also feel sorry for the fact that their dog has had to suffer the upheaval of being rehomed (and perhaps worse, since some rescued dogs have undoubtedly been abused or neglected). These understandable human emotions can result in a rescued dog being overwhelmed with too much love and affection, which can result in an already insecure dog becoming very clingy. This can lead to the development of separation anxiety problems, which can take a very long time to overcome (see Chapter Six). To avoid these problems, don't try to compensate for your rescued Cocker's past experiences by spoiling him, but concentrate on giving him space to settle into your home in his own time. Be calm and patient but try to get into a normal routine as soon as possible, treating your new dog as if he's always been a member of your family. Encourage him to spend short periods of time alone (activity toys, such as stuffed Kongs, may help with this), and try not to let him follow you everywhere when you are at home. This approach will help your new Cocker settle into your home as quickly and easily as possible.

CAR TRAVEL

Most Cockers love car travel, but some puppies may initially be travel sick, so don't take your puppy out in the car immediately after a meal or your puppy may be sick and will start to associate car travel with feeling nauseous. Similarly, if your puppy only travels in the car to go to the vet for his injections, this can cause a negative association to develop. Avoid this by taking your puppy on lots of short journeys (even if you don't go anywhere in particular), and then gradually build up the length of the journey as time goes by.

It is not safe to allow your puppy to travel loose in the car, so you should ensure he is secure, either by using a harness that attaches to the car's rear seat-belt fixings or by using a travel crate. Some owners prefer to have their dog travel in the boot space, behind a dog guard, but this offers little protection to the dog in the case of a rear shunt. There have been incidents where the rear car door has opened after impact, causing dogs travelling behind a guard to be flung into the road with disastrous results.

THE BEST OF CARE

Chapter 5

As the owner of a Cocker Spaniel, you must be dedicated to providing the best possible care for your dog throughout his life. You need to provide a nourishing, well-balanced diet, you need to keep his coat in good order, and you need to provide an exercise programme that is suitable for your Cocker's age and lifestyle.

FEEDING YOUR COCKER

Choosing the right food for your Cocker can seem impossibly complicated due to the huge range of commercially prepared dog foods on the market and the wide range of opinions on what constitutes a healthy diet for a dog. The following information will hopefully help you make an informed decision on what diet would best suit your Cocker.

BASIC CANINE NUTRITION

Dogs need certain essential nutrients to thrive, and the best way of ensuring that your dog gets these nutrients is to feed a balanced diet containing the right proportions of proteins, fats, carbohydrates, vitamins and minerals and water.

WATER

Water is the most important nutrient in a dog's diet. A dog can go for several days without food, but can become quickly dehydrated after only a few hours in hot weather without water. Fresh water in a clean bowl should always be freely available for your Cocker. This is especially important if you feed a dry complete food, which contains little moisture.

PROTEINS

Proteins are necessary for every aspect of a dog's growth and development, and they also provide calories for energy. To be accurate, dogs do not need the actual proteins but the essential amino acids contained within the proteins.

Essential amino acids are those that dogs cannot produce within their own bodies, so they must be consumed in their diet. The best-quality proteins are those that contain the highest percentage of essential amino acids, and those that are most easily digested by the dog (proteins that are not easily digested will be lost in the dog's faeces). Eggs provide the best-quality source of protein, but red meat, chicken and fish are also excellent sources. Other sources of protein, such as cereals/grains, are of a lower quality, meaning they are harder to digest. A side effect of feeding your dog a diet with high cereal content is the production of larger and more frequent amounts of faeces due to the relative indigestibility of lower-quality protein sources.

Protein is essential for growth and development, and also provides calories for energy.

FATS
Contrary to popular opinion, fat is not a bad thing and is an important part of a healthy dog's diet. Fats supply energy, transport fat-soluble vitamins around the body, and contain essential fatty acids, which are required for many aspects of good health, such as maintaining coat and skin condition. Fats also make a food more palatable, which is a necessary part of canine nutrition (a diet that no dog wants to eat is not a good diet). Sources of fats include animal fats, fish oils and vegetable oils. An excess of fat in the diet can lead to obesity, a common problem in dogs today, and other related disorders, so you must be careful not to feed your Cocker a diet too high in fat for his daily needs.

CARBOHYDRATES
Carbohydrates are present in most commercially prepared dog foods, but whether they are actually needed by the dog and, if so, in what quantity, is the subject of some debate. Carbohydrates can be divided into two types: digestible (sugars/starches) and non-digestible (fibre).

Starchy carbohydrates are found in cereals such as rice, oats, wheat and corn, all widely used in commercial and home-prepared dog diets, as, once cooked, they are relatively inexpensive and provide a source of energy for the dog. However, as with fats and proteins, if a dog is fed a diet too high in carbohydrates for his energy needs, there is a high risk of obesity and related conditions. Some dogs are also unable to

tolerate starchy carbohydrates, resulting in intestinal problems.

Fibre is not considered to be an essential nutrient for dogs, but it is found in most commercially prepared dog foods and is thought to be beneficial for bowel health, promoting good stool formation. It is also used in weight-reduction programmes, as high-fibre diets provide bulk, making the dog feel 'full' without any extra calories. Common sources of fibre include bran, beet pulp and pectin.

VITAMINS & MINERALS
Vitamins are needed in small, balanced amounts for a variety of essential body functions, such as regulating the dog's metabolism and assisting in the chemical reactions essential for energy to be released from digested food. Most

of the vitamins needed by a dog must be provided in the diet, as they cannot be naturally produced in their bodies. Vitamins are defined as fat-soluble (able to be stored by the body in the liver and fatty tissues) and water-soluble (not able to be stored by the body so must be consumed on a frequent basis). Fat-soluble vitamins include A, D, K and E, and water-soluble vitamins include B and C.

Dogs also require about 20 minerals, such as calcium, phosphorous, potassium, sodium and iron, which are needed for bone and muscle formation, controlling fluid balances and maintaining a healthy nervous system.

FEEDING FOR LIFE

A dog's nutritional needs may change over different stages of his life, so it is important that his diet is adjusted to reflect those differing requirements. For example, a Cocker puppy needs relatively large amounts of food in proportion to his bodyweight to supply his body with the energy it needs during this period of rapid growth and development. This food also needs to contain higher levels of essential nutrients than are required once he is fully grown. Adult Cockers may also have differing nutritional needs depending on how active their lifestyle is. For example, a working Cocker who lives in an outside kennel and works during the shooting season will need greater quantities of food, with higher levels of proteins and fats (for energy), than a pet Cocker who lives in a centrally heated home and receives only moderate exercise. Neutering may also have a significant effect on an adult Cocker's nutritional needs; many an owner has found that their neutered Cocker becomes prone to weight gain and so requires a diet that is not too high in protein, fat or carbohydrate.

Senior/veteran Cockers (over 10 years) also tend to be less active than in their youth and so become more prone to putting on excess weight, which can have a damaging effect on the joints and on the heart. A veteran Cocker may need considerably less food than an active young dog and that food needs to be lower in protein, fat and carbohydrate but higher in fibre (so the dog still feels satisfied after eating). Some veteran dogs with serious conditions such as diabetes, liver or kidney disease will often need to be fed a special diet under veterinary supervision.

A working Cocker will need to be fed very differently from the average pet Cocker.

THE BREEDER'S CHOICE

Good breeders will supply new owners with a small amount of the food the puppy is used to eating. This food will usually have been chosen by the breeder because it suits his/her own dogs and keeps them in optimum condition. For this reason, many owners will rely on their breeder's experience and continue feeding the same diet to their own puppy with equally good results. However, there may be reasons why you feel you would like to change your puppy's food. Perhaps the breeder's food is not widely available in your area, is too expensive for your budget, or you would prefer to feed a different type of diet (e.g. a BARF diet instead of a commercial complete food). If so, you should always try to keep your puppy on the diet he is used to for at least a week or two while he settles into your home. Then introduce changes to his diet very slowly and gradually, a little at a time over a period of seven to 10 days. If you are tempted to rush this, your puppy could suffer from an upset stomach whereas a slow introduction to a new diet gives your puppy's digestive system time to adjust naturally.

Complete diets are formulated to meet the differing needs of dogs throughout their lifetimes.

DIETARY CHOICES

There are many ways of providing a dog with the nutrients he needs, but remember: there is no one diet that suits every single dog at every stage of his life. Your Cocker is an individual and the best diet for him is the one he enjoys and which suits his current energy requirements, at a price you can afford.

COMPLETE

A complete dry dog food aims to provide a balanced diet containing all the essential nutrients a dog needs in the form of a dry kibble. Complete foods are extremely popular with Cocker breeders and owners because of their convenience. No preparation is needed; you just scoop your dog's meal allowance straight from the bag into his bowl. Many owners also add small amounts of meat or fish, although complete foods are, in theory, designed to be fed alone.

If you decide that a complete food is the right diet for your Cocker, choose one with the appropriate protein content for his needs. For example, a puppy needs a high-protein food, but an older Cocker does not. A complete food suitable for puppies would usually contain 25-30 per cent protein whereas a food suitable for the average adult Cocker would contain around 18-20 per cent protein. A Cocker Spaniel, being a relatively small breed, is normally fully grown by eight or nine months, so it is not normally necessary to continue feeding a high-protein puppy food much beyond this age.

Make sure you choose a complete food made with high-quality ingredients. Look at the ingredient list on the bag and check that there is a good-quality protein source (such as chicken, fish or lamb) listed first. Foods that list cereals first (e.g. maize, corn, wheat) have a high cereal content, which makes them much cheaper, but more of this food will have to be consumed by your dog in order for him to obtain the

With canned food, it is important to check the label so you can work out what ingredients are included.

If you are feeding a home-made diet, you need to ensure that your Cocker is getting the essential nutrients he requires.

nutrients he needs. He will also produce more faeces due to the less easily digestible content. You may also want to check the ingredient list for artificial colourings and flavourings since these are often included in cheaper complete diets. However, these supplements are designed to appeal to owners rather than their dogs; your Cocker does not want or need his kibble to be all the colours of the rainbow. There is anecdotal evidence that too many artificial additives in complete foods can contribute to hyperactive/disturbed behaviour in dogs as they do in children.

CANNED

Canned dog food may be designed to be fed alone as a complete food, or as a complementary food to be fed with a carbohydrate mixer biscuit. Canned foods are often very palatable to dogs, but, as with complete foods, it pays to read the labels and look for high-quality ingredients. Some canned pet foods contain artificial colourings and flavourings and also have a high sugar content, which can have a detrimental effect on your dog's dental health. Canned foods also have a high water content (around 75 per cent) meaning they could be considered a relatively uneconomic way of feeding your dog.

If you have a Cocker who prefers to eat a wet diet, there are now alternatives to canned food, which consist of ingredients such as cooked meat, rice, vegetables, vitamins and minerals, sealed into plastic vacuum packs. These may be a better alternative for your Cocker if you have concerns about the quality of ingredients in some canned foods.

HOME-MADE

There is no reason why you cannot choose to feed your Cocker a home-made diet in the traditional way. Some care is needed to ensure your dog receives a balanced diet of all the essential nutrients, but feeding a home-prepared diet does give owners total control over what goes into their food, and many believe that a freshly prepared diet is a more natural, and therefore healthier, option than a commercial diet. A home-prepared diet would usually involve feeding fresh meat with a biscuit-based mixer or rice perhaps (to provide the carbohydrate element), sometimes with the addition of vegetables (for their vitamin content and to provide roughage). To ensure a home-made diet contains all the essential vitamins and minerals, a multivitamin supplement should be added, but only at the stated dose since excess vitamin supplementation can prove harmful to the dog.

You would be advised to ask your vet for advice on home-prepared diets, to check that you are providing all the nutrients needed.

BARF

BARF is an acronym for Biologically Appropriate Raw Food or Bones And Raw Food. This diet is becoming increasingly popular with owners who believe that commercially prepared dog foods are not appropriate for a species that evolved to eat a raw, natural diet containing meat and bones. They believe changing from processed dog foods to a totally raw diet has many benefits for the dog, including better dental health, better stool formation, improved coat and skin condition, and fewer health problems generally. However, it is true to say that many in the veterinary profession are not convinced by these arguments so it remains a somewhat controversial subject. If you are interested in feeding BARF to your Cocker, it would be sensible to do as much research as possible and invest in at least one book on the subject, which will explain what you need to do to ensure your

dog receives a balanced raw diet. However, note that the BARF philosophy aims for an overall balanced diet rather than a complete and balanced diet at every meal (the complete food philosophy).

FEEDING REGIME

Puppies have small stomachs, but they need to eat relatively large amounts of food in proportion to their bodyweight. This means their food should be split into several small meals spread throughout the day, rather than the one or two meals an adult dog can expect to receive. From eight weeks to four months, a puppy should ideally be fed four meals a day, and these meals should be at least four hours apart so that there is time for the pup to digest his food before it is time for his next meal. From four to six months of age, you can reduce the number of meals down to three a day, and from six months old, your puppy will usually be ready to go down

to two meals a day. Traditionally, owners would give their dog one meal a day from 12 months old, but many Cocker owners find their dogs are happier continuing on two meals a day for the rest of their lives.

HOW MUCH TO FEED

Every Cocker is an individual, so it is simply not possible to recommend a fixed amount of food that every dog will require at a particular stage of his life. This applies as much to puppies as it does to adult dogs; some Cocker puppies will need rather more food than others to maintain their appropriate bodyweight and growth levels. If you choose to feed your Cocker a complete food, it is tempting to follow to the letter the amounts recommended by the manufacturer, but these are only guidelines to be used as a rough starting point. Your hands and eyes are better able to tell you whether you are feeding your dog the right amount. You should be

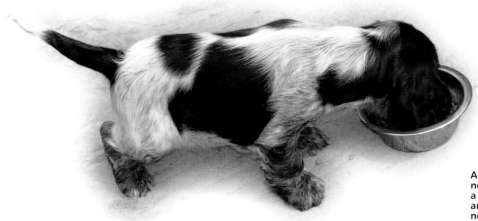

A puppy will need four meals a day when he arrives in his new home.

It is all too easy for a Cocker to pile on the pounds, so keep a close check on your dog's weight. You should be able to feel the ribs, but not see them.

able to feel your Cocker's ribs easily but not see them, and he should have a waist. If this is the case, you are feeding exactly the right amount of food. If you have trouble feeling the ribs through a layer of fat, then you need to cut down the food; if the ribs are too visible and feel prominent, your dog is underweight and you need to increase his food. If your Cocker has a thick coat, especially if he is a puppy carrying a lot of puppy fluff, it can look as if he is overweight. However, this can be an optical illusion caused by the hair, so you will need to feel under the coat to check he is carrying the right amount of bodyweight.

FREE FEEDING

Some commercial dog food manufacturers recommend free feeding, where food is left down all day for a dog to eat whenever he feels hungry. However, this could encourage a dog to eat more than he needs to maintain optimum bodyweight and so contribute to obesity. It is also not practical in homes where there is more than one dog, as the owner will not be able to keep track of how much food is being consumed by which dog. Another problem with free feeding a puppy is that it makes house training more challenging, since a free-fed puppy's digestive system is constantly active, making it difficult for an owner to know when the pup needs to toilet. A puppy fed at scheduled meal times will need to toilet immediately after eating, which is something an owner can use to their advantage when training.

GROOMING

Grooming is a very important part of Cocker ownership, and should never become a problem as long as you and your dog get used to regular grooming sessions right from the start.

PUPPY GROOMING

Start grooming your puppy from the day you collect him. Spend just a few minutes gently brushing him all over, including his legs and ears; get him used to lying on his back while you brush underneath him, paying particular attention to under the elbows. If you start this routine early on, when your puppy has very little coat, it will be much easier to get him to accept regular, thorough grooming when he is an adult. You should also practise grooming your puppy on a raised surface or table, making sure the surface is non-slip by placing a rubber mat or piece of carpet on the top first. This will make grooming much easier when your puppy is older and has more coat to keep tidy. Never try to groom your puppy on the floor; you will find it impossible to get your pup to stand still and will probably end up giving yourself backache in the process!

As your puppy gets older, the coat will start to grow thicker and longer, and feathering will start to develop on the legs, ears and under the chest and tummy. This thick hair is known as puppy fluff

GROOMING KIT

A basic Cocker Spaniel grooming kit would include the following items:
- Bristle brush
- Slicker brush (rectangular or square brush with angled metal pins)
- Wide-toothed comb and/or comb with rotating teeth (for combing feathering and removing knots)
- Narrow-toothed comb (often called a spaniel comb)
- Small pair of straight-edged scissors (for trimming hair around feet and inside ears etc)
- Nail clippers.

If you decide to trim your own dog, you may also want to consider the following additional items:
- Coat King (stripping tool for pet Cockers only, not show dogs)
- Thinning scissors
- Clippers.

and some puppies will grow more than others, depending on their breeding. At this stage, a quick brush will no longer be sufficient; you must be prepared to spend at least 10-15 minutes a day thoroughly grooming your Cocker. Use a comb to go through the feathering, and a slicker brush to remove dead hair from the top coat along the body, and to work through small tangles in the feathering. You can also use your scissors to keep the feet neat and tidy, cutting the hair away from underneath the pads and around the outside of the foot. You could also trim away excess hair growing

around the entrance to the ear canal.

PROFESSIONAL TRIMMING

Many Cocker owners choose to employ a professional groomer for trimming, but this is not essential. If you decide to use a groomer, you will need to book an appointment every eight weeks or so, from the age of six to eight months, with a first, short session to tidy up feet, ears etc recommended at about four months old. This short session at four months old will help prepare your puppy for longer visits to the groomer once he is older.

HAND-STRIPPING

The traditional way to trim a Cocker is known as 'hand-stripping', whereby puppy fluff or dead hair is stripped away using a comb and finger and thumb. This is a time-consuming process but it leaves a natural, long-lasting finish. However, the art of hand-stripping is more often carried out by breeders of show Cockers rather than by grooming parlours, so you may find it difficult to locate anyone offering such a service. If you intend showing your Cocker, it should be mentioned that hand-stripping is essential (clipping a show Cocker is frowned upon!). If you plan to hand-strip your puppy, you will need to be patient, as puppy fluff will not come out until it is ready – your puppy may be

GROOMING A COCKER SPANIEL

Groom your puppy for a few minutes every day so that he gets used to the routine.

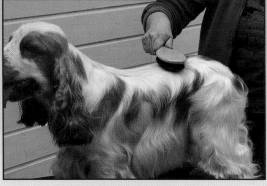
Use a bristle brush to work through the body coat.

A slicker brush will remove dead hair and help to keep the coat tangle-free.

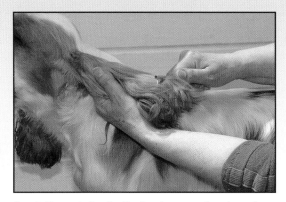
Comb through the feathering to prevent mats and tangles forming.

eight months old, or even older, before his coat is ready to strip.

CLIPPING
Many dog groomers (i.e. high-street grooming parlours) will trim Cockers using electric clippers over the head and body. Some do a very smart job, leaving the dog with sufficient feathering so that it still resembles a Cocker Spaniel; others practise what can only be described as 'sheep-shearing', shaving the dog from head to toe,

which can look very unattractive to say the least! Some dog groomers will offer a compromise between clipping and hand-stripping; they remove excess coat using thinning scissors and stripping tools. This does not take as long as hand-stripping and will produce a more natural effect than clipping. It should be stressed that sometimes clipping is the only viable option if, for example, grooming has been severely neglected, resulting in a coat that is badly matted.

The best way to find a good groomer is by personal recommendation. Ask your breeder to recommend a groomer, or if you see a nicely trimmed Cocker in your neighbourhood, ask the owner where they take their dog. Once you have found a groomer you are comfortable with, make sure they understand the style of trimming you want. If you don't want your Cocker's hair cut too short, you need to inform the groomer before he/she starts work.

HAND-STRIPPING

For the best effect, the dead hair is pulled out using finger and thumb.

The hair is pulled from the head to achieve a smooth outline.

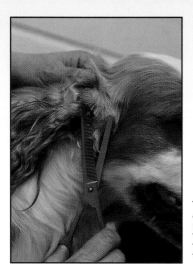

Moving down to the shoulder, the aim is for the coat to lie close to the body.

The hair is pulled along the length of the back for a smooth topline.

TRIMMING

The art of trimming is to neaten the appearance, while still giving a natural look.

Thinning scissors are used to remove some of the hair behind the ears, so that the ears lie flat.

The hair on the throat and chest is thinned out.

The feathering on the front legs needs to be tidied up.

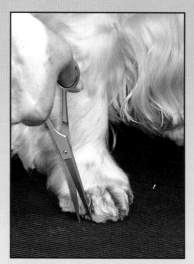

The hair growing around the feet is trimmed to give a neat, cat-like appearance.

The 'trousers' at the rear are given a tidy up.

The feathering on the underside is trimmed to a smooth contour.

The finished result: Groomed to perfection for the show ring.

LEARNING TO TRIM YOUR COCKER

Although many Cocker owners prefer to use the services of a professional dog groomer, it is quite possible for you to trim your own dog. Learning this skill takes time and practice but many owners find it very relaxing, plus they save the expense of going to a professional groomer. If you are interested in learning to trim your own dog, the best way is to find someone who is willing to give you practical tuition on a one-to-one basis. If you are interested in hand-stripping and/or show presentation, you could ask your breeder if they can help you or if they can recommend another breeder who provides this service. If you are more interested in learning how to keep a pet Cocker neat and tidy, you may find a local college or grooming parlour that offers basic courses aimed at pet owners rather than professional groomers. There are also grooming videos/DVDs available, which demonstrate grooming techniques and can be helpful for a pet owner who is unable to find personal tuition.

NEUTERING AND COCKER COATS

It is worth mentioning that once a Cocker is neutered (whether a dog or bitch), the coat will often change texture and become thicker and woollier, necessitating more frequent grooming and trimming. This coat change means that neutered dogs cannot usually be hand-stripped, so electric clippers are often the easiest option.

NB: This does not mean that you should not have your Cocker neutered, merely that you should be aware of this side effect.

WORKING COCKERS AND COAT CARE

Many working Cockers do not grow as much coat and feathering as their show-type cousins (excess coat would be a hindrance when working), so grooming requirements will not usually be so great. However, working Cocker puppies should still be trained to accept grooming from an early age, as regular brushing and combing will still be necessary to help keep the coat clean and tangle-free. Some trimming of the feet and ears may also be necessary to keep them neat and tidy. Some owners of working dogs with thicker coats also clip their dogs' coats short for easy maintenance.

BATHING

Many Cocker owners wonder how often they should bath their dog, but there is no set rule. You should bath your dog when you think he needs it, depending on how dirty he looks and how much dog odour you can tolerate! Frequent bathing will not damage your dog's coat as long as you use a proprietary dog shampoo, which is formulated not to strip the oil from the coat. You may also find that using a conditioner after shampooing makes your Cocker's coat easier to groom afterwards and less prone to tangle.

When you bath your Cocker, use a non-slip rubber mat in the basin/bath to help your dog feel more secure and to stop his feet from slipping. Make sure you rinse well after shampooing and/or conditioning.

TEETH

Just like us, dogs need attention paid to their dental care. Oral disease is one of the most common problems that vets see in dogs. This is largely due to commercial dog diets, which tend to be too soft and contain sugars, leading to a build-up of plaque and tartar on the teeth. Such problems can be minimised by regularly brushing your dog's teeth. Use a toothbrush and toothpaste formulated for pets (not human toothpaste, which is intended to be spat out – dogs can't spit!).

Ideally, you should aim to brush your Cocker's teeth daily, or at least every other day. Start by getting your puppy used to you rubbing your finger around his teeth and gums, and then introduce a toothbrush once he is used to your finger. You can also give your Cocker chew toys, which will encourage him to use his teeth and so help remove plaque at the same time. Many owners also like to give occasional recreational bones to help keep their dog's teeth clean. These bones should be given raw and they must be big and hard enough so that the Cocker cannot eat them easily (marrow and knuckle bones are ideal for this purpose).

NAILS

If you have trained your puppy to accept regular handling of his feet and nails, you should be able to trim your own Cocker's nails

ROUTINE CARE

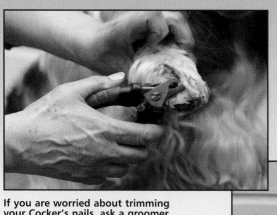

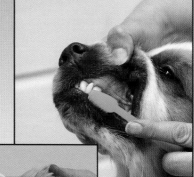

Teeth will need regular cleaning.

If you are worried about trimming your Cocker's nails, ask a groomer or a vet to show you what to do.

It is essential to check your Cocker's ears and to clean them when necessary.

quite easily with clippers, although some owners prefer to ask their groomer or vet to carry out this task. When clipping a dog's nails, it can be difficult to know how much to take off. However, if you trim the tips regularly, it will keep nails short without the risk of taking too much off and cutting into the quick.

If you have a Cocker with dewclaws (situated inside the front legs just above the foot), don't forget to check these nails, as they can be hidden by leg hair and, if neglected, can curl round and penetrate the skin of the leg, causing pain and infection.

EARS

Ear care is essential in the Cocker Spaniel, as in all breeds with long, floppy ears. You should check the insides of the ear regularly; the visible part should be clean and pink, with no signs of discharge, although a little brown wax is fairly common and nothing to worry about, unless excessive. A healthy ear canal needs access to fresh air, so you need to ensure there is no excess hair blocking the entrance to the ear canal; use your scissors to trim any excess growth on a regular basis. Clean the visible part inside the ear, if necessary, using a small pad of cotton wool and a proprietary ear

lotion (although many breeders swear by using rubbing alcohol – surgical spirits – for cleaning ears). There is also an old-fashioned ear powder (Thornit), which Cocker owners and breeders have long used to prevent ear trouble and kill ear mites. Thornit is not a licensed veterinary product, but nevertheless it is often very effective, particularly if your Cocker is troubled with itchy, smelly ears.

Never poke or attempt to clean down the ear canal with a cotton bud, as this could cause injury.

You should consult your vet immediately if there is any smelly

Cocker puppies are full of energy, but too much exercise can damage vulnerable joints.

discharge, or if your dog is continually scratching his ears or shaking his head, as this could indicate an infection or penetration of the ear by a grass seed. Exercising in long grass in summer can cause problems for a Cocker, as it is easy for a grass seed to be picked up in the ears or in the feathering on the legs. If these are not removed promptly (by thorough grooming), they can penetrate the ear canal (or other parts of the body) and cause enormous problems, necessitating urgent veterinary treatment. Some Cocker owners use snoods on their Cocker's ears to prevent such problems.

EXERCISE
Your Cocker will need regular exercise to keep him happy and

healthy – making sure your dog leads an active life, with play sessions and daily walks, will help to prevent him becoming overweight (and will help your waistline, too!).

PUPPIES
New owners of Cocker puppies are often surprised by the lively nature of their new arrival, and seek to 'tire out' their pup by going for long walks, thinking to themselves that their puppy will know when it is time to stop. Unfortunately, this practice can be quite dangerous to a puppy's health because over-exercise can cause damage to immature joints and growth plates, resulting in conditions such as early arthritis. Too much exercise when young may also be a contributory factor

in the development of diseases such as hip dysplasia (see Chapter Eight).

A good rule of thumb is to allow five minutes of exercise for every month of your puppy's age until he is fully grown. So if your Cocker is four months old, his walks should not last longer than 20 minutes at a time. Two short walks a day, combined with normal play sessions in the garden, are quite enough for such a young puppy. As your pup gets older, you can gradually increase the length of his walks, still following the five-minute rule until he is fully grown at around nine or 10 months of age. This does not mean that at 10 months old, you should immediately start taking your puppy for long hikes, but you can start to go for longer

A long country ramble, with plenty of interesting scents is a Cocker's idea of heaven.

walks at this age, gradually building up the length over the next few months.

As well as restricting the length of walks for your puppy, you should prevent him from running up and down stairs or jumping high in the air (e.g. to catch a toy), as this could also damage his joints.

ADULTS

Once your Cocker is a fully mature adult, he will take as much exercise as you can give him, although he is also very adaptable and will happily accept two moderate daily walks during the week, with slightly longer walks at the weekend (in addition to play sessions in the garden). On average, an adult Cocker will need at least half an hour's walk twice a day (more if you have a working Cocker). These daily walks should include some free-running exercise off the lead (once you have trained a satisfactory recall), as there is nothing a Cocker likes more than to run free and use his spaniel nose to follow as many interesting smells as possible.

Try to vary your daily walks and not follow exactly the same route to the same park, day in and day out, as this can become boring for your dog (and you). If you vary your walking routes, this will also help reduce the risk of your Cocker becoming territorial over a particular area, which can sometimes happen if dogs are exercised in the same place every day. If you walk your Cocker Spaniel in rural areas, you should keep him on the lead when walking close to farm animals or other livestock.

LONG WALKS

If you do intend taking your Cocker on long-distance hikes, do remember to build up to long walks gradually over a period of months; don't expect your Cocker to cope with a 10-mile hike up a mountain if he is only used to half an hour in the local park twice a day.

Cockers have a strong instinct to retrieve, and playing in the water makes it even more fun.

SWIMMING

Cockers are usually natural water babies, and will need very little encouragement to jump into the nearest muddy puddle or stream. They are generally quick learners when it comes to swimming, but some may need time to get used to the idea, particularly in deeper water, like a lake or the sea.

Swimming is excellent exercise for dogs since it enables them to work nearly all their muscles without putting strain on joints, especially useful if your dog is recovering from an injury or needs to lose a lot of weight. There are now many specialised canine hydrotherapy pools, which offer swimming facilities in a controlled, safe environment for dogs recovering from illness/injuries or for owners who wish to build up their dog's general fitness and stamina but don't have access to a natural, safe swimming area. As with any other form of exercise, you need to start slowly and gently build up swimming sessions for your dog over time.

PLAY SESSIONS

In addition to regular daily walks, play sessions with your Cocker will keep his mind and body active, and will also help build a closer bond between you and your dog. Playing with your dog and making him use his brain at the same time can be as tiring for him as taking him for a walk, something to bear in mind if formal walks must be limited (e.g. if you have a young puppy). Here are some suggestions for games you can play with your Cocker.

- **Retrieving:** Many Cockers have a natural instinct to carry and retrieve objects, so a game of fetch will use those instincts and help exercise his body at the same time. Teaching your puppy to retrieve reliably can take time and patience, as most will be happy to chase after a

Stand back! When a Cocker Spaniel shakes, it's time to take cover...

ball or toy but will not necessarily want to bring it back to you! A good method is to have two or more toys in your pocket so you can throw one (just a few feet to begin with) and give praise when your pup chases after it, then use an excited voice to show your pup the second toy, which usually makes your pup run straight back to you. You then throw the second toy and while your pup is chasing it, pick up the first so you always have another toy to throw. Keep sessions short to begin with, as puppies cannot concentrate for long, and always use special toys that your puppy really likes but doesn't have access to all the time (to maintain his interest).

• **Hide-and-seek:** This game can be played in the garden or inside the house on a wet day. You will need to teach your Cocker a reliable Sit-stay first (an exercise covered in most puppy training classes). When this has been mastered, tell your puppy to sit and stay, then go and find a good hiding place. Once you've found one, call your pup in an excited voice and let him find you, offering a tasty treat when he is successful.

• **Find the treat/toy:** This is another game that can be played inside or outside. Tell your Cocker to sit and stay, then go and hide some tasty treats in a variety of different hiding places before telling him to "Go find". Your Cocker will have fun using his nose to sniff out the treats (make sure you use high-value treats that you know your dog really loves). This game can also be adapted so you use a favourite toy rather than edible treats (for those dogs who are not particularly motivated by food). Reward your dog with a play session with his toy when he successfully finds it.

An older Cocker will probably feel more comfortable if his coat is clipped.

CARING FOR THE OLDER COCKER

Old age comes at different times depending on the individual dog. There are Cockers who remain energetic and quite youthful up to 10 years old and beyond, whereas others may be starting to slow down by this time. The signs that your Cocker may be showing his age include stiffness when moving in the morning, sleeping more, hearing loss, fading eyesight, and skin/coat changes. Elderly Cockers are prone to fatty lumps in the skin. These lumps are generally non-malignant lipomas and can be safely left alone unless they are irritating the dog. However, lumps should always be checked out by your vet as a precaution. While it is normal for an older Cocker's skin to become drier in texture, if the skin condition is very poor,

with patches of hair loss, then consult your vet, as this could indicate an easily treated thyroid problem, which is not uncommon in the older Cocker.

You can give your Cocker a comfortable old age by making sure he is fed a good-quality diet and is not allowed to become overweight. Although an older dog may not want, or be able to go for long walks, he should still be exercised regularly to keep his joints moving and to help keep his weight down. If your Cocker is showing signs of joint stiffness, you can supplement the diet with glucosamine chondroitin and/or fish oil. Old dogs feel the cold more, so a soft, cosy bed, away from draughts, is a must. You may also find your Cocker will appreciate a warm, waterproof coat for walks in cold/damp weather.

Be patient if your Cocker suffers an occasional lapse in house training; an old dog may not have such good bladder or bowel control as he once had. Take your elderly dog for regular veterinary check-ups to ensure any changes to his health can be assessed and treated where appropriate,

It is common for older dogs to lose interest in toys and games to some extent, but just like ageing humans, mental stimulation is needed to keep the brain active. Make the effort to play a game, or practise a training exercise with your older Cocker on a regular basis to keep him interested in life. If your dog is showing signs of becoming mentally confused, consult your vet, as there are now drugs and supplements available that can help the senile dog.

SAYING GOODBYE

Sadly, there will come a time when you realise that your old Cocker is no longer enjoying life as he once did, either because of illness or pain, or simply because of old age. When to say goodbye is the hardest decision any pet owner will ever have to make, but providing a dignified, peaceful end is also the greatest kindness we can do for a much-loved canine friend. Discuss the situation with your vet, who will be able to give advice and suggest any viable treatment options. But don't expect the vet to make the final decision of whether the dog should be put to sleep.

The signs that the time has come to make that decision are when the bad days far outweigh the good, and when you can see your Cocker has little interest in life anymore, or is in pain more often than he is not. You may find he loses his appetite and shows a reluctance to move out of his bed during the day; he may not wag his tail and greet you with enthusiasm as he once did. Sometimes owners understandably delay the inevitable because they cannot bear to lose their beloved Cocker, but listen to what your dog is telling you, and have the strength to say goodbye when the time is right for him.

In time, you will be able to look back and remember all the happy times you spent with your beloved Cocker Spaniel.

TRAINING AND SOCIALISATION

Chapter 6

When you decided to bring a Cocker Spaniel into your life, you probably had dreams of how it was going to be: long walks together, cosy evenings with a Cocker lying devotedly at your feet, and whenever you returned home, there would always be a special welcome waiting for you.

There is no doubt that you can achieve all this – and much more – with a Cocker, but like anything that is worth having, you must be prepared to put in the work. A Cocker Spaniel, regardless of whether he is a puppy or an adult, does not come ready trained, understanding exactly what you want and fitting perfectly into your lifestyle. A Cocker has to learn his place in your family and he must discover what is acceptable behaviour.

We have a great starting point in that the Cocker has an impeccable temperament, which is why he is a wonderful companion. A Cocker is gentle and affectionate, yet he has a *joie de vivre* and an exuberance, which makes him a fun dog to own. He is outward going, intelligent and eager to please.

THE FAMILY PACK

Dogs have been domesticated for some 14,000 years, but, luckily for us, they have inherited and retained behaviour from their distant ancestor – the wolf. A Cocker Spaniel may never have lived in the wild, but he is born with the survival skills and the mentality of a meat-eating predator who hunts in a pack. A wolf living in a pack owes its existence to mutual co-operation and an acceptance of a hierarchy, as this ensures both food and protection. A domesticated dog living in a family pack has exactly the same outlook. He wants food, companionship, and leadership – and it is your job to provide for these needs.

YOUR ROLE

Theories about dog behaviour and methods of training go in and out of fashion, but in reality, nothing has changed from the day when wolves ventured in from the wild to join the family circle. The wolf (and equally the dog) accepts a subservient place in the family pack in return for food and protection. In a dog's eyes, you are his leader, and he relies on you to make all the important decisions. This does not mean that you have to act like a dictator or a bully. You are accepted as a leader, without argument, as long as you have the right credentials.

The first part of the job is easy. You are the provider, and you are therefore respected because you supply food. In a Cocker's eyes, you must be the ultimate hunter because a day never goes by when you cannot find food. The second

Can you be a firm, fair and consistent leader?

part of the leader's job description is straightforward, but for some reason we find it hard to achieve. In order for a dog to accept his place in the family pack he must respect his leader as the decision-maker. A low-ranking pack animal does not question authority; he is perfectly happy to see someone else shoulder the responsibility. Problems will only arise if you cut a poor figure as leader and the dog feels he should mount a challenge for the top-ranking role.

HOW TO BE A GOOD LEADER
There are a number of guidelines to follow to establish yourself in the role of leader in a way that your Cocker understands and respects. If you have a puppy, you may think you don't have to take this on board for a few months, but that would be a big mistake. Start as you mean to go on, and your pup will be quick to find his place in his new family.

- **Keep it simple:** Decide on the rules you want your Cocker to obey and always make it 100 per cent clear what is acceptable, and what is unacceptable, behaviour.
- **Be consistent:** If you are not consistent about enforcing rules, how can you expect your Cocker to take you seriously? There is nothing worse than allowing your Cocker to jump up at you one moment and then scolding him the next time he does it because you are wearing your best clothes. As far as the Cocker is concerned, he may as well try it on because he can't predict your reaction.
- **Get your timing right:** If you are rewarding your Cocker, and equally if you are reprimanding him, you must respond within one to two seconds otherwise the dog will not link his behaviour with your reaction (see page 90).

- **Read your dog's body language:** Find out how to read body language and facial expressions (see page 90) so that you understand your Cocker's feelings and his intentions.
- **Be aware of your own body language:** You can help your dog to learn by using your body language to communicate with him. For example, if you want your dog to come to you, open your arms out and look inviting. If you want your dog to stay, use a hand signal (palm flat, facing the dog) so you are effectively 'blocking' his advance. Remember, the Cocker is a highly intelligent dog, and has an uncanny knack of knowing your moods and your intentions before you have given out any obvious signals. For this reason, you must always try to keep one step ahead, and try to see the world from your dog's perspective.
- **Tone of voice:** Dogs are very receptive to tone of voice, so you can use your voice to praise him or to correct undesirable behaviour. If you are pleased with your Cocker, praise him to the skies in a warm, happy voice. If you want to stop him raiding the bin, use a deep, stern voice when you say "No".
- **Give one command only:** If you keep repeating a command, or keeping changing it, your Cocker will think you are babbling and will probably ignore you. If your Cocker does not respond the first time you ask, make it simple by using a treat to lure him into position, and then you can reward him for a correct response.

Give clear signals so your Cocker understands what you want.

- **Daily reminders:** A young, excitable Cocker is apt to forget his manners from time to time, and an adolescent dog may attempt to challenge your authority (see page 99). Rather than coming down on your Cocker like a ton of bricks when he does something wrong, try to prevent bad manners by daily reminders of good manners. For example:
  i Do not let your dog barge ahead of you when you are going through a door.
  ii Do not let your Cocker leap out of the car the moment you open the door (which could be potentially lethal, as well as being disrespectful).
  iii Do not let him eat from your hand when you are at the table.
  iv Do not let him 'win' a toy at the end of a play session and then make off with it. You 'own' his toys, and you must end every play session on your terms. If your Cocker takes possession of a toy, do not confront him, demanding that he gives up the toy. This may fuel his

determination to keep it. The best plan is to trade with him, substituting something equally desirable – a tasty piece of cheese or sausage – so that your Cocker is happy to give up his toy. In this way, you have won the battle without the need for conflict.

UNDERSTANDING YOUR COCKER

Body language is an important means of communication between dogs, which they use to make friends, to assert status, and to avoid conflict. It is important to get on your dog's wavelength by understanding his body language and reading his facial expressions.

- A positive body posture and a wagging tail indicate a happy, confident dog. The Cocker is famous for his ever-wagging tail and busy manner. Owners say you know something is wrong if your Cocker is lying still…

- A crouched body posture with ears back and tail down show that a dog is being submissive. A dog may do this when he is being told off or if a more assertive dog approaches him.
- A bold dog will stand tall, looking strong and alert. His ears will be forward and his tail will be held high.
- A dog who raises his hackles (lifting the fur along his topline) is trying to look as scary as possible. This may be the prelude to aggressive behaviour, but, in many cases, the dog is apprehensive and is unsure how to cope with a situation.
- A playful dog will go down on his front legs while standing on his hind legs in a bow position. This friendly invitation says: "I'm no threat, let's play."
- A dominant, aggressive dog will meet other dogs with a hard stare. If he is challenged, he may bare his teeth and growl, and the corners of his mouth will be drawn forward. His ears

will be forward and he will appear tense in every muscle (see page 108).
- A nervous dog will often show aggressive behaviour as a means of self-protection. If threatened, this dog will lower his head and flatten his ears. The corners of his mouth may be drawn back, and he may bark or whine.

GIVING REWARDS

Why should your Cocker do as you ask? If you follow the guidelines given above, your Cocker should respect your authority, but what about the time when he is playing with a new doggy friend or has found a really enticing scent? The answer is that you must always be the most interesting, the most attractive, and the most irresistible person in your Cocker's eyes. It would be nice to think you could achieve this by personality alone, but most of us need a little extra help. You need to find out what is the biggest reward for your dog, and

If you observe two dogs interacting with each other, you will begin to understand canine body language.

to give it when he does as you ask. Generally speaking, parti-colours are great foodies, and will do anything you ask for a tasty treat. However, solids are not so food-orientated, and are therefore harder to motivate. In some cases, a Cocker may take to a particular toy, and you can use that as a special reward, which you only bring out at training sessions.

When you are teaching a dog a new exercise, you should reward your Cocker frequently. When he knows the exercise or command, reward him randomly so that he keeps on responding to you in a positive manner. If your dog does something extra special, like leaving his canine chum mid-play in the park, make sure he really knows how pleased you are by giving him a handful of treats or throwing his ball a few extra times. If he gets a bonanza reward, he is more likely to come back on future occasions, because you have proved to be even more rewarding than his previous activity.

You need to find out what motivates your Cocker so you can give him a reward he values.

TOP TREATS
Some trainers grade treats depending on what they are asking the dog to do. A dog may get a low-grade treat, such as a piece of dry food, to reward good behaviour on a random basis, such as sitting when you open a door or allowing you to examine his teeth. But high-grade treats, which may be cooked liver, sausage or cheese, are reserved for training new exercises or for use in the park when you want a really good recall. Whatever type

of treat you use, remember to subtract it from your Cocker's daily ration. Fat Cockers are lethargic, prone to health problems, and will almost certainly have a shorter life expectancy. Reward your Cocker, but always keep a check on his figure!

HOW DO DOGS LEARN?
It is not difficult to get inside your Cocker's head and understand how he learns, as it is not dissimilar to the way we learn. Dogs learn by conditioning: they find out that specific behaviours produce specific

consequences. This is known as operant conditioning or consequence learning. Consequences have to be immediate or clearly linked to the behaviour, as a dog sees the world in terms of action and result. Dogs will quickly learn if an action has a bad consequence or a good consequence.

Dogs also learn by association. This is known as classical conditioning or association learning. It is the type of learning made famous by Pavlov's experiment with dogs. Pavlov presented dogs with food and measured their salivary response

THE CLICKER REVOLUTION

Karen Pryor pioneered the technique of clicker training when she was working with dolphins. It is very much a continuation of Pavlov's work and makes full use of association learning.

Karen wanted to mark 'correct' behaviour at the precise moment it happened. She found it was impossible to toss a fish to a dolphin when it was in mid-air, when she wanted to reward it. Her aim was to establish a conditioned response so the dolphin knew that it had performed correctly and a reward would follow.

The solution was the clicker: a small matchbox-shaped training aid, with a metal tongue that makes a click when it is pressed. To begin with, the dolphin had to learn that a click meant that food was coming. The dolphin then learnt that it

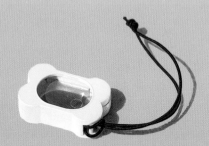

must 'earn' a click in order to get a reward. Clicker training has been used with many different animals, most particularly with dogs, and it has proved hugely successful. It is a great aid for pet owners and is also widely used by professional trainers who train highly specialised skills.

(how much they drooled). Then he rang a bell just before presenting the food. At first, the dogs did not salivate until the food was presented. But after a while they learnt that the sound of the bell meant that food was coming, and so they salivated when they heard the bell. A dog needs to learn the association in order for it to have any meaning. For example, a dog that has never seen a lead before will be completely indifferent to it. A dog that has learnt that a lead means he is going for a walk will get excited the second he sees the lead; he has learnt to associate a lead with a walk.

BE POSITIVE

The most effective method of training dogs is to use their ability to learn by consequence and to teach that the behaviour you want produces a good consequence. For example, if you ask your Cocker to "Sit", and reward him with a treat, he will learn that it is worth his while to sit on command because it will lead to a treat. He is far more likely to repeat the behaviour, and the behaviour will become stronger, because it results in a positive outcome. This method of training is known as positive reinforcement, and it generally leads to a happy, co-operative dog

that is willing to work, and a handler who has fun training their dog.

The opposite approach is negative reinforcement. This is far less effective and often results in a poor relationship between dog and owner. In this method of training, you ask your Cocker to "Sit", and, if he does not respond, you deliver a sharp yank on the training collar or push his rear to the ground. The dog learns that not responding to your command has a bad consequence, and he may be less likely to ignore you in the future. However, it may well have a bad consequence for you, too. A dog that is treated in this way may associate harsh handling with the handler and become aggressive or fearful. Instead of establishing a pattern of willing co-operation, you are establishing a relationship built on coercion.

GETTING STARTED

As you train your Cocker, you will develop your own techniques as you get to know what motivates him. You may decide to get involved with clicker training or you may prefer to go for a simple command-and-reward formula. It does not matter what form of training you use, as long as it is based on positive, reward-based methods.

There are a few important guidelines to bear in mind when you are training your Cocker:

- Find a training area that is free from distractions, particularly when you are just starting out.
- Keep training sessions short, especially with young puppies that have very short attention spans.
- Do not train if you are in a bad mood or if you are on a tight schedule – the training session will be doomed to failure. The Cocker has a stubborn streak, and you need to keep the mood relaxed and happy to get the best results.
- If you are using a toy as a reward, make sure it is only available when you are training. In this way it has an added value for your Cocker.
- If you are using food treats, which is the best training aid for most Cocker Spaniels, make sure they are bite-size and easy to swallow; you don't want to

Cockers cannot resist an interesting scent, so try to find a training area that is free from temptations.

hang about while your Cocker chews on his treat.
- All food treats must be deducted from your Cocker's daily food ration.
- When you are training, move around your allocated area so that your dog does not think that an exercise can only be performed in one place.
- If your Cocker is finding an exercise difficult, try not to get frustrated. Go back a step and praise him for his effort. You will probably find he is more successful when you try again at the next training session. Many

owners say training a Cocker is a case of taking one step forward, and two steps back, so you will need to be patient.
- Always end training sessions on a happy, positive note. Ask your Cocker to do something you know he can do – it could be a trick he enjoys performing – and then reward him with a few treats or an extra-long play session.

In the exercises that follow, clicker training is introduced and followed, but all the exercises will work without the use of a clicker.

INTRODUCING A CLICKER

This is dead easy and the Cocker, who loves his food, will learn about the clicker in record time! It can be combined with attention training, which is a very useful tool and can be used on many different occasions.

- Prepare some treats and go to an area that is free from distractions. When your Cocker stops sniffing around and looks at you, click and reward by throwing him a treat. This means he will not crowd you, but will go looking for the treat. Repeat a couple of times. If your Cocker is very easily distracted, you may need to start this exercise with the dog on a lead.

- After a few clicks, your Cocker understands that if he hears a click, he will get a treat. He must now learn that he must 'earn' a click. This time, when your Cocker looks at you, wait a little longer before clicking, and then reward him. If your Cocker is on a lead but responding well, try him off the lead.

- When your Cocker is working for a click and giving you his attention, you can introduce a cue or command word, such as "Watch". Repeat a few times, using the cue. You now have a Cocker that understands the clicker and will give you his attention when you ask him to "Watch".

TRAINING EXERCISES

THE SIT

This is the easiest exercise to teach, so it is rewarding for both you and your Cocker.

- Choose a tasty treat and hold it just above your puppy's nose. As he looks up at the treat, he will naturally go into the Sit. As soon as he is in position, reward him.
- Repeat the exercise, and when your pup understands what you want, introduce the "Sit" command.
- You can practise at mealtimes by holding out the bowl and waiting for your dog to sit. Most Cockers learn this one very quickly!

THE DOWN

Work hard at this exercise because a reliable Down is useful in many different situations, and an instant Down can be a lifesaver.

- You can start with your dog in a Sit, or it is just as effective to teach it when the dog is standing. Hold a treat just below your puppy's nose, and slowly lower it towards the ground. The treat acts as a lure, and your puppy will follow it,

Use a treat to lure your Cocker into the Sit.

If you lower a treat to the ground, your Cocker will follow it with his nose and lower himself into the Down.

Make yourself sound exciting so your Cocker wants to come to you.

first going down on this forequarters, and then bringing his hindquarters down as he tries to get the treat.

- Make sure you close your fist around the treat, and only reward your puppy with the treat when he is in the correct position. If your puppy is reluctant to go Down, you can apply gentle pressure on his shoulders to encourage him to go into the correct position.
- When your puppy is following the treat and going in to position, introduce a verbal command.
- Build up this exercise over a period of time, each time waiting a little longer before giving the reward, so the puppy learns to stay in the Down position.

THE RECALL

It is never too soon to start training the Recall. In fact, if you have a puppy it is best to start almost from the moment the puppy arrives home, as he has a strong instinct to follow you. Make sure you are always happy and excited when your Cocker comes to you, even if he has been slower than you would like. Your Cocker Spaniel must believe that the greatest reward is coming to you.

- You can start teaching the Recall from the moment your puppy arrives home. He will naturally follow you, so keep calling his name and rewarding him every time he comes to you.

- Practise in the garden. When your puppy is busy exploring, get his attention by calling his name, and as he runs towards you, introduce the verbal command "Come". Make sure you sound happy and exciting, so your puppy wants to come to you. When he responds, give him lots of praise.
- If your puppy is slow to respond, try running away a few paces, or jumping up and down. It doesn't matter how silly you look, the key issue is to get your puppy's attention, and then make yourself irresistible!
- In a dog's mind, coming when called should be regarded as the best fun because he knows he is always going to be

rewarded. Never make the mistake of telling off your Cocker Spaniel, no matter how slow he is to respond, as you will undo all your previous hard work.

- When you are free running your dog, make sure you have his favourite toy, or a pocket full of treats so you can reward him at intervals throughout the walk when you call him to you. Do not allow your dog to free run and only call him back at the end of the walk to clip on his lead. An intelligent Cocker Spaniel will soon realise that the Recall means the end of his walk, and then end of fun – so who can blame him for not wanting to come back?

TRAINING LINE

This is the equivalent of a very long lead, which you can buy at a pet store, or you can make your own with a length of rope. The training line is attached to your Cocker's collar and should be around 15 feet (4.5 metres) in length.

The purpose of the training line is to prevent your Cocker from disobeying you so that he never has the chance to get into bad habits. For example, when you call your Cocker and he ignores you, you can immediately pick up the end of the training line and call him again. By picking up the line you will have attracted his attention, and if you call in an excited, happy voice, your Cocker will come to you. The moment he comes to you, give him a tasty treat so he is instantly rewarded for making the 'right' decision.

The training line is very useful when your Cocker becomes an adolescent and is testing your leadership. When you have reinforced the correct behaviour a number of times, your dog will build up a strong recall and you will not need to use a training line.

WALKING ON A LOOSE LEAD

This is a simple exercise, which baffles many Cocker owners. In most cases, owners are too impatient, wanting to get on with the expedition rather that training the dog how to walk on a lead. Take time with this one; a Cocker that pulls on the lead is no pleasure to own.

SECRET WEAPON

You can build up a strong Recall by using another form of association learning. Buy a whistle, and when you are giving your Cocker his food, peep on the whistle. You can choose the type of signal you want to give: two short peeps or one long whistle, for example. Within a matter of days, your dog will learn that the sound of the whistle means that food is coming.

Now transfer the lesson outside. Arm yourself with some tasty treats and the whistle. Allow your Cocker to run free in the garden, and, after a couple of minutes, use the whistle. The dog has already learnt to associate the whistle with food, so he will come towards you. Immediately reward him with a treat and lots of praise. Repeat the lesson a few times in the garden so you are confident that your dog is responding before trying it in the park. Make sure you always have some treats in your pocket when you go for a walk, and your dog will quickly learn how rewarding it is to come to you.

- In the early stages of lead training, allow your puppy to pick his route and follow him. He will get used to the feeling of being 'attached' to you, and has no reason to put up any resistance.
- Next, find a toy or a tasty treat and show it to your puppy. Let him follow the treat/toy for a few paces, and then reward him.
- Build up the amount of time your pup will walk with you, and when he is walking nicely by your side, introduce the verbal command "Heel" or "Close". Give lots of praise when your pup is in the correct position.
- When your pup is walking alongside you, keep focusing his attention on you by using his name, and then rewarding him when he looks at you. If it is going well, introduce some changes of direction.
- Do not attempt to take your puppy out on the lead until you have mastered the basics at home. You need to be confident that your puppy accepts the lead and will focus his attention on you when requested, before you face the challenge of a busy environment.
- As your Cocker gets bigger, he may try to pull on the lead, particularly if you are heading somewhere he wants to go, such as the park. If this happens, stop, call your dog to you, and do not set off again until he is in the correct position. It may take time, but your Cocker will eventually realise that it is more productive to walk by your side, than to pull ahead.

With practice, your Cocker will learn to walk on a loose lead.

STAYS

This may not be the most exciting exercise, but it is one of the most useful. There are many occasions when you want your Cocker to stay in position, even if it is only for a few seconds. The classic example is when you want your Cocker to stay in the back of the car until you have clipped on his lead. Some trainers use the verbal command "Stay" when the dog is to stay in position for an extended period of time, and "Wait" if the dog is to stay in position for a few seconds until you give the next command. Others trainers use a universal "Stay" to cover all situations. It all comes down to personal preference, and as long as you are consistent, your dog will understand the command he is given.

- Put your puppy in a Sit or a Down, and use a hand signal (flat palm, facing the dog) to show he is to stay in position. Step a pace away from the dog. Wait a second, step back and

Build up the Stay exercise in stages, gradually extending the distance you can leave your dog.

reward him. If you have a lively pup, you may find it easier to train this exercise on the lead.

- Repeat the exercise, gradually increasing the distance you can leave your dog. When you return to your dog's side, praise him quietly, and release him with a command, such as "OK".

- Remember to keep your body language very still when you are training this exercise, and avoid eye contact with your dog. Work on this exercise over a period of time, and you will build up a really reliable Stay.

SOCIALISATION

While your Cocker is mastering basic obedience exercises, there is other, equally important, work to do with him. A Cocker is not only becoming a part of your home and family, he is becoming a member of the community. He needs to be able to live in the outside world, coping calmly with every new situation that comes his way. It is your job to introduce him to as many different experiences as possible, and encourage him to behave in an appropriate manner.

In order to socialise your Cocker effectively, it is helpful to understand how his brain is developing, and then you will get a perspective on how he sees the world.

CANINE SOCIALISATION (Birth to 7 weeks)

This is the time when a dog learns how to be a dog. By interacting with his mother and his siblings, a pup learns about leadership and submission. He learns to read body posture so that he understands the intentions of his mother and littermates. A puppy that is taken away from his litter too early may always have behavioural problems with other dogs, either being fearful or aggressive.

SOCIALISATION PERIOD (7 to 12 weeks)

This is the time to get cracking and introduce your Cocker puppy to as many different experiences as possible. This includes meeting different people, other dogs and animals, seeing new sights, and hearing a range of sounds, from the vacuum cleaner to the roar of traffic. At this stage, a puppy learns very quickly and what he learns will stay with him for the rest of his life. This is the best time for a puppy to move to a new home, as he is adaptable and ready to form deep bonds.

FEAR-IMPRINT PERIOD (8 to 11 weeks)

This occurs during the socialisation period, and it can be the cause of problems if it is not handled carefully. If a pup is exposed to a frightening or painful experience, it will lead to lasting impressions. Obviously, you will attempt to avoid frightening situations, such as your pup being bullied by a mean-spirited older dog, or a firework going off, but you cannot always protect your puppy from the unexpected. If your pup has a nasty experience, the best plan is to make light of it and distract him by offering him a treat or a game. The pup will take the lead from you and will be reassured that there is nothing to worry about. If you mollycoddle him and sympathise with him, he is far more likely to retain the memory of his fear.

SENIORITY PERIOD (12 to 16 weeks)

During this period, your Cocker puppy starts to cut the apron strings and becomes more independent. He will test out his status to find out who is the pack leader: him or you. Bad habits, such as play biting, which may have been seen as endearing a few weeks earlier, should be firmly discouraged. Remember to use positive, reward-based training, but make sure your puppy knows that you are the leader and must be respected.

SECOND FEAR-IMPRINT PERIOD (6 to 14 months)

This period of socialisation is not as critical as the first fear-imprint

Puppies are very impressionable, and what your puppy experiences during his first year of life will have a lasting effect on his personality.

period, but it should still be handled carefully. During this time your Cocker may appear apprehensive, or he may show fear of something familiar. You may feel as if you have taken a backwards step, but if you adopt a calm, positive manner, your Cocker will see that there is nothing to be frightened of. Do not make your dog confront the thing that frightens him. Simply distract his attention, and give him something else to think about, such as obeying a simple command, such as "Sit" or "Down". This will give you the opportunity to praise and reward your dog, and will help to boost his confidence.

YOUNG ADULTHOOD AND MATURITY (1 to 4 years)

The timing of this phase depends on the size of the dog: the bigger the dog, the later it is. This period coincides with a dog's increased size and strength, mental as well as physical. Some dogs, particularly those with a dominant nature, will test your leadership again and may become aggressive towards other dogs. Firmness and continued training are essential at this time so that your Cocker accepts his status in the family pack.

IDEAS FOR SOCIALISATION

When you are socialising your Cocker Spaniel, you want him to experience as many different situations as possible. Try out some of the following ideas, which will ensure that your Cocker has an all-round education.

If you are taking on a rescued dog and have little knowledge of his background, it is important to work through a programme of socialisation. A young puppy soaks up new experiences like a sponge, but an older dog can still learn. If a rescued dog shows fear or apprehension, treat him in exactly the same way as you would treat a youngster who is going through the second fear-imprint period (see page 99).

Take your Cocker Spaniel out and about so that he learns to adapt to a variety of different situations.

- Accustom your puppy to household noises, such as the vacuum cleaner, the television and the washing machine.
- Ask visitors to come to the door, wearing different types of clothing – for example, wearing a hat, a long raincoat, or carrying a stick or an umbrella.
- If you do not have children at home, make sure your Cocker has a chance to meet and play with them. Go to a local park and watch children in the play area. You will not be able to take your Cocker inside the play area, but he will see children playing and will get used to their shouts of excitement.
- Attend puppy classes. These are designed for puppies between the ages of 12 to 20 weeks, and give puppies a chance to play and interact together in a controlled, supervised environment. Your vet will have details of a local class.
- Take a walk around some quiet streets, such as a residential area, so your Cocker can get used to the sound of traffic. As he becomes more confident, progress to busier areas.
- Go to a railway station. You don't have to get on a train if you don't need to, but your Cocker will have the chance to experience trains, people wheeling luggage, loudspeaker announcements, and going up and down stairs and over railway bridges.
- If you live in the town, plan a trip to the country. You can enjoy a day out and provide an opportunity for your Cocker to

Give your Cocker the opportunity to meet other dogs of sound temperament.

see livestock, such as sheep, cattle and horses.
- One of the best places for socialising a dog is at a country fair. There will be crowds of people, livestock in pens, tractors, bouncy castles, fairground rides and food stalls.
- When your dog is over 20 weeks of age, find a training class for adult dogs. You may find that your local training class has both puppy and adult classes.

TRAINING CLUBS
There are lots of training clubs to choose from. Your vet will probably have details of clubs in your area, or you can ask friends who have dogs if they attend a club. Alternatively, use the internet to find out more information. But how do you know if the club is any good?

Before you take your dog, ask if you can observe a class and find out the following:
- What experience does the instructor(s) have?
- Do they have experience with Cocker Spaniels?
- Is the class well organised, and are the dogs reasonably quiet? (A noisy class indicates an unruly atmosphere, which will not be conducive to learning.)
- Are there are a number of classes to suit dogs of different ages and abilities?
- Are positive, reward-based training methods used?
- Does the club train for the Good Citizen Scheme (see page 109).

If you are not happy with the training club, find another one. An inexperienced instructor who cannot handle a number of dogs in a confined environment can do more harm than good.

THE ADOLESCENT COCKER
It happens to every dog – and every owner. One minute you have an obedient, well-behaved youngster, and the next you have a moody adolescent who appears to have forgotten everything he learnt. This applies equally to males and females, although the type of adolescent behaviour, and its onset, varies between individuals.

In most cases a Cocker will hit adolescence at around nine months, and you can expect behavioural changes for at least a couple of months. All Cockers are individuals, but it appears that females can be harder to handle during the adolescent period than males. While a male may become disobedient, a female is more likely to have mood swings. She may be moody as she comes into season, and again about nine weeks later when she would have been producing puppies. With luck, your Cocker will grow up and show signs of becoming a mature adult dog by 12 to 14 months. In reality, adolescence is not the nightmare period you may imagine, if you see it from your Cocker's perspective.

Just like a teenager, an adolescent Cocker feels the need to flex his muscles and challenge the status quo. He may become disobedient and break house rules as he tests your authority and your role as leader. Your response must be firm, fair and consistent. If you show that you are a strong leader (see page 88) and are quick to reward good behaviour, your

Cocker will accept you as his protector and provider. Remember, boredom is the enemy, and if your Cocker lacks mental stimulation, his behaviour will deteriorate as he find ways to amuse himself. It is your job to provide sufficient exericise and training to keep a young, intelligent dog well occupied.

The biggest mistake a Cocker owner can make is to humanise the dog and treat him like a baby. Instead of trying to put human feelings on to a dog, an owner should try to imagine what it is like from the dog's perspective. A dog does not understand complex issues; he wants to live within boundaries that are set for him.

WHEN THINGS GO WRONG

Positive, reward-based training has proved to be the most effective method of teaching dogs, but what happens when your Cocker does something wrong and you need to show him that his behaviour is unacceptable? The old-fashioned school of dog training used to rely on the powers of punishment and negative reinforcement. A dog who raided the bin, for example, was smacked. Now we have learnt that it is not only unpleasant and cruel to hit a dog, it is also ineffective. If you hit a dog for stealing, he is more than likely to see you as the bad

The Cocker is a highly intelligent animal, and, as he matures, he may try to challenge your authority.

There are times when life is full of excitement and a Cocker becomes 'deaf' to your calls.

consequence of stealing, so he may raid the bin again, but probably not when you are around. If he raided the bin some time before you discovered it, he will be even more confused by your punishment, as he will not relate your response to his 'crime'.

A more commonplace example is when a dog fails to respond to a recall in the park. When the dog eventually comes back, the owner puts the dog on the lead and goes straight home to punish the dog for his poor response. Unfortunately, the dog will have a different interpretation. He does not think: "I won't ignore a recall command because the bad consequence is the end of my play in the park." He thinks: "Coming to my owner resulted in the end of playtime – therefore coming to my owner has a bad consequence, so I won't do that again."

There are a number of strategies to tackle undesirable behaviour – and they have nothing to do with harsh handling.

Ignoring bad behaviour: A lot of undesirable behaviour in young Cockers is learnt from their owners. It is so easy to hype up an excitable youngster, and most owners don't even know they are doing it. For example, visitors come to the door, and you make a great fuss, calling the dog, restraining him, telling him off for barking or jumping up. Before you know it, your Cocker has learnt that the arrival of visitors is the signal for anarchy; he will match your mood, becoming more and more hyped up, and you have lost your position of authority. If your Cocker becomes demanding and attention-seeking, the best plan is to take all the tension out of the situation and ignore him. Do not look at him,

do not speak to him, and do not push him down – all these actions are rewarding for your Cocker. But someone who turns their back on him and offers no response is plain boring. The moment your Cocker stops barking, and has four feet on the ground, give him lots of praise and maybe a treat. If you repeat this often enough, the Cocker will learn that jumping up and barking does not have any good consequences, such as getting attention. Instead he is ignored. However, when he is quiet and has all four feet on the ground, he gets loads of attention. He links the action with the consequence, and chooses the action that is most rewarding. You will find that this strategy works well with all attention-seeking behaviour, such as whining or scrabbling at doors. Being ignored is a worst-case scenario for a Cocker, so remember to use it as an effective training tool.

Stopping bad behaviour: There are occasions when you want to call an instant halt to whatever it is your Cocker is doing. You may have caught him red-handed stealing food from the kitchen counter – although you will have to be quick, as Cockers are highly accomplished thieves. But in this instance, your dog has already committed the 'crime', so your aim is to stop him and to redirect his attention. You can do this by using a deep, firm tone of voice to say "No", which will startle him, then call him to you in a bright, happy voice. If necessary, attract him with a toy or a treat. The moment your Cocker stops the undesirable behaviour and comes towards you, you can reward his good behaviour. You can back this up by running through a couple of simple exercises, such as a Sit or a Down, and rewarding with treats. In this way, your Cocker focuses his attention on you, and sees you as the greatest source of reward and pleasure.

In a more extreme situation, when you want to interrupt undesirable behaviour, and you know that a simple "No" will not do the trick, you can try something a little more dramatic. If you get a can and fill it with pebbles, it will make a really loud noise when you shake it or throw it. The same effect can be achieved with purpose-made training discs. The dog will be startled and stop what he is doing. Even better, the dog will not associate the unpleasant noise with you. This gives you the perfect opportunity to be the nice guy, calling the dog to you and giving him lots of praise.

PROBLEM BEHAVIOUR

If you have trained your Cocker from puppyhood, survived his adolescence and established yourself as a fair and consistent leader, you will end up with a brilliant companion dog. The well-balanced, out-going Cocker is eager to please; he thrives on company, both human and canine, and likes nothing better than spending time with his owners.

However, problems may arise unexpectedly, or you may have taken on a rescued Cocker with behavioural issues. Problems are often created by the type of owner who treats the dog as a human, forgetting the dog has this own needs and limitations. Dogs can be inappropriately punished and become sensitised to gestures such as a raised hand. The owner may fail to realise the significance of what has happened, because it can take as little as one incident for every learned response. This is particularly the case when there is delayed punishment that is out of proportion to what the dog is doing, or punishment when the dog has issued a mild challenge e.g. by growling when the owner approaches after the dog has stolen something. In this situation, the dog may become defensive, which could result in aggressive behaviour. The owner, however, is not aware that the dog has become fearful of them and is wary of being approached/held by the collar or looked at.

The Cocker has an outstanding temperament, but if you ever feel you cannot cope with your dog's behaviour, do not delay in seeking professional advice.

In recent times, there has been a lot of publicity given to dogs with Canine rage syndrome. This is very rare condition where a dog may attack a person, without provocation and without warning, and then appear to have no knowledge or memory of what has just taken place. If rage syndrome is diagnosed, it is very distressing for the owner of the dog, and there may be no solution, barring euthanasia. The cause of the condition has yet be discovered, and it is therefore the responsibility of breeders to ensure that dogs showing any signs of rage syndrome are not bred from. Many people have confused rage syndrome with bad temperament. They are not the same. Rage syndrome is an unprovoked outburst of aggression. Bad temperament is a different matter.

If you are worried about your Cocker and feel out of your depth, do not delay in seeking professional help. This is readily available, usually through a referral from your vet, or you can find out additional information on the internet (see Appendices for web addresses). An animal behaviourist will have experience in tackling problem behaviour and will be able to help both you and your dog.

JEALOUSY

As with most problems, this need never become an issue if you handle your Cocker correctly from day one. However, some Cockers, if allowed, may become overly attached to one person, and then become jealous if anyone else has dealings with their chosen person. This can be a result of poor temperament, which can happen when puppies, such as golden-coloured Cockers, are mass produced by unscrupulous breeders, purely for profit. But it can also happen if the tendency to be jealous or possessive has not been instantly curbed.

In all cases, prevention is better than cure. When a Cocker puppy arrives in the family, make sure all family members are involved in his daily care, sharing out the tasks, such as grooming, feeding, exercising and training. In this way, the Cocker values all members of his family and does not focus on an individual. If this has not happened, and a Cocker shows signs of jealousy, the chosen person must try to ignore the dog, and allow other family members to care for him. This can be very difficult for both parties, but it is the only way the dog will learn that he does not have the right to 'own' a person, and must respond equally to the people he lives with.

SEPARATION ANXIETY

The Cocker Spaniel loves his family, and so it is important that he learns to accept short periods of separation without becoming anxious. A new puppy should be left for short periods on his own, ideally in a crate where he cannot get up to any mischief. It is a good idea to leave him with a boredom-busting toy (see page 53) so he will be happily occupied in your absence. When you return, do not rush to the crate and make a huge fuss. Wait a few minutes, and then calmly go to the crate and release your dog, telling him how good he has been. If this scenario is repeated a number of times, your

Use a baby gate to accustom your Cocker to being on his own – but still within sight of you.

Cocker will soon learn that being left on his own is no big deal. As your Cocker grows up, keep to the routine of making minimum fuss when you leave the house, and ignoring your Cocker for a few minutes when you return. In this way, your Cocker learns to accept comings and goings as a matter of course.

Problems with separation anxiety are most likely to arise if you take on a rescued dog who has major insecurities. You may also find your Cocker hates being left if you have failed to accustom him to short periods of isolation when he was growing up. Separation anxiety is expressed in a number of ways, and all are equally distressing for both dog and owner. An anxious dog who is left alone may bark and whine continuously, urinate and defecate,

and may be extremely destructive.

There are a number of steps you can take when attempting to solve this problem.

- Put up a baby-gate between adjoining rooms, and leave your dog in one room while you are in the other room. Your dog will be able to see you and hear you, but he is learning to cope without being right next to you. Build up the amount of time you can leave your dog in easy stages.
- Buy some boredom-busting toys and fill them with some tasty treats. Whenever you leave your dog, give him a food-filled toy so that he is busy while you are away.
- If you have not used a crate before, it is not too late to start. Make sure the crate is big and

comfortable, and train your Cocker to get used to going in his crate while you are in the same room. Gradually build up the amount of time he spends in the crate, and then start leaving the room for short periods. When you return, do not make a fuss of your dog. Leave him for five or 10 minutes before releasing him so that he gets used to your comings and goings.
- Pretend to go out, putting on your coat and jangling keys, but do not leave the house. An anxious dog often becomes hyped up by the ritual of leave taking, and so this will help to desensitize him.
- When you go out, leave a radio or a TV on. Some dogs are comforted by hearing voices and background noise when they are left alone.
- Try to make your absences as short as possible when you are first training your dog to accept being on his own. When you return, do not fuss your dog, rushing to his crate to release him. Leave him for a few minutes, and when you go to him remain calm and relaxed so that he does not become hyped up with a huge greeting.

If you take these steps, your dog should become less anxious, and, over a period of time, you should be able to solve the problem. However, if you are failing to make progress, do not delay in calling in expert help.

ASSERTIVE BEHAVIOUR

If you have trained and socialised your Cocker correctly, he will

An assertive Cocker may show guarding behaviour and become possessive over his food or a toy.

know his place in the family pack and will have no desire to challenge your authority. As we have seen, adolescent dogs test the boundaries, and this is the time to enforce all your earlier training so your Cocker accepts that he is not top dog.

Cockers were bred to be biddable, but they are clever dogs, and males, in particular, may become assertive as they mature. This often happens if early training has been neglected, or if you have allowed your adolescent Cocker to rule the roost. Behavioural issues may also occur if you have taken on a rescued dog who has not been trained and socialised.

Assertive behaviour e is expressed in many different ways, which may include the following:

- Showing lack of respect for your personal space. For example, your dog will barge through doors ahead of you or jump up at you.
- Getting up on to the sofa or your favourite armchair, and growling when you tell him to get back on the floor.
- Becoming possessive over a toy, or guarding his food bowl by growling when you get too close.
- Growling when anyone approaches his bed or when anyone gets too close to where he is lying.
- Ignoring basic obedience commands.
- Showing no respect to younger members of the family, pushing amongst them, and completely ignoring them.
- Male dogs may start marking (cocking their leg) in the house.

- Aggression towards people (see page 108).

If you see signs of your Cocker becoming too assertive, you must work at lowering his status so that he realises that you are the leader and he must accept your authority. Although you need to be firm, you also need to use positive training methods so that your Cocker is rewarded for the behaviour you want. In this way, his 'correct' behaviour will be strengthened and repeated.

There are a number of steps you can take to lower your Cocker's status. They include:

- Go back to basics and hold daily training sessions. Make sure you have some really tasty treats, or find a toy your Cocker really values and only bring it out at training sessions. Run

through all the training exercises you have taught your Cocker. Make a big fuss of him and reward him when he does well. This will reinforce the message that you are the leader and that it is rewarding to do as you ask.
- Teach your Cocker something new; which could be learning a trick, such as shaking paws. Having something new to think about will mentally stimulate your Cocker, and he will benefit from interacting with you.
- Be 100 per cent consistent with all house rules – your Cocker must never sit on the sofa, and you must never allow him to jump up at you.
- If your Cocker has been guarding his food bowl, put the bowl down empty, and drop in a little food at a time. Periodically stop, and tell your

Channel your Cocker's energy in a positive way, such as playing retrieve, so you can reward desirable behaviour.

The Good Citizen Scheme is aimed at training dogs to be well-behaved members of the community.

energies. However, if your Cocker is still seeking to be assertive, or you have any other concerns, do not delay in seeking the help of an animal behaviourist.

AGGRESSION

Aggression is a complex issue, as there are different causes and the behaviour may be triggered by numerous factors. It may be directed towards people, but far more commonly it is directed towards other dogs. Aggression in dogs may be the result of:

- Assertive behaviour (see page 106).
- Defensive behaviour: This may be induced by fear, pain or punishment.
- Territory: A dog may become aggressive if strange dogs or people enter his territory (which is generally seen as the house and garden).
- Intra-sexual issues: This is aggression between sexes – male-to-male or female-to-female.
- Parental instinct: A mother dog may become aggressive if she is protecting her puppies.

Cocker to "Sit" and "Wait". Give it a few seconds, and then reward him by dropping in more food. This shows your Cocker that you are the food provider, and he can only eat when you allow him to.

- Make sure the family eats before you feed your Cocker. Some trainers advocate eating in front of the dog (maybe just a few bites from a biscuit) before starting a training session, so the dog appreciates your elevated status.

- Do not let your Cocker barge through doors ahead of you, or leap from the back of the car before you release him. You may need to put your dog on the lead and teach him to "Wait" at doorways, and then reward him for letting you go through first.
- If your Cocker is progressing well with his retraining programme, think about getting involved with a dog sport, such as agility or competitive obedience. This will give your Cocker a positive outlet for his

A dog who has been well socialised (see page 98) and has been given sufficient exposure to other dogs at significant stages of his development will rarely be aggressive. A well-bred Cocker that has been reared correctly should not have a hint of aggression in his temperament. Obviously if you have taken on an older, rescued dog, you will have little or no knowledge of his background, and if he shows signs of aggression, the cause will need to be determined. In most cases, you would be well advised to call in professional help if you see aggressive behaviour in your dog; if the aggression is directed towards people, you should seek immediate advice. This behaviour can escalate very quickly and could lead to disastrous consequences.

HYPERACTIVITY

The Cockers is a merry, active dog, which is their great charm, but you do not want a Cocker who crosses the line and becomes hyperactive. A hyperactive dog will bark and whine continuously, will rush around the house, and will rarely sleep.

There are generally two reasons why a Cocker behaves in this way
- Firstly, an unwitting owner may have purchased a working Cocker, and fails to cater for his mental and physical needs. If a dog of this type is under-exercised, and has no mental stimulation, he may find the only outlet for his energy is in inappropriate, hyperactive behaviour. One solution is to rehome the dog where it has the opportunity to work. If this is considered undesirable, or is not feasible, the owner will need to introduce radical lifestyle changes so the dog is no longer under-exercised and bored, and will change his behaviour.
- The other cause of hyperactivity is feeding a complete diet that is too high in protein for a dog's physical needs. It is also important to be aware of E numbers in the diet, as this can have an adverse effect on some dogs.

NEW CHALLENGES

If you enjoy training your Cocker, you may want to try one of the many dog sports that are now on offer.

GOOD CITIZEN SCHEME

This is a scheme run by the Kennel Club in the UK and the American Kennel Club in the USA. The schemes promote responsible ownership and help you to train a well-behaved dog who will fit in with the community. The schemes are excellent for all pet owners, and they are also a good starting point if you plan to compete with your Cocker when he is older. The KC and the AKC schemes vary in format. In the UK there are three levels: bronze, silver and gold, with each test becoming progressively more demanding. In the AKC scheme there is a single test.

Some of the exercises include:
- Walking on a loose lead among people and other dogs.
- Recall amid distractions.
- A controlled greeting where dogs stay under control while owners meet.
- The dog allows all-over grooming and handling by his owner, and also accepts being handled by the examiner.
- Stays, with the owner in sight, and then out of sight.
- Food manners, allowing the owner to eat without begging, and taking a treat on command.
- Sendaway – sending the dog to his bed.

The tests are designed to show the control you have over your dog, and his ability to respond correctly and remain calm in all situations. The Good Citizen Scheme is taught at most training clubs. For more information, log on to the Kennel Club or AKC website (see Appendices).

SHOWING

In your eyes, your Cocker is the most beautiful dog in the world – but would a judge agree? Showing is a highly competitive sport and as the Cocker is so popular, classes tend to be very big. However, many owners are bitten by the showing bug, and their calendar is governed by the dates of the top showing fixtures.

Showing is highly competitive, but it can be very rewarding.

COMPETITIVE OBEDIENCE

Border Collies and German Shepherds dominate this sport, but gundogs have also made their mark at the highest level. In the USA, a greater variety of breeds are trained for competitive obedience, and there is no reason why the Cocker should not have a go. He has the intelligence; the challenge is motivating your Cocker and focusing his attention. The classes start off being relatively easy and become progressively more challenging with additional exercises and the handler giving minimal instructions to the dog.

Exercises include:

- Heelwork: Dog and handler must complete a set pattern on and off the lead, which includes left turns, right turns, about turns, and changes of pace.
- Recall: This may be when the handler is stationary or moving.
- Retrieve: This may be a dumbbell or any article chosen by the judge.
- Sendaway: The dog is sent to a designated spot and must go into an instant Down until he is recalled by the handler.
- Stays: The dog must stay in the Sit and in the Down for a set amount of time. In advanced classes, the hander is out of sight.
- Scent: The dog must retrieve a single cloth from a pre-arranged pattern of cloths that has his owner's scent, or, in advanced classes, the judge's scent. There may also be decoy cloths.
- Distance control: The dog must execute a series of moves (Sit, Stand, Down) without moving from his position and with the handler at a distance.

Even though competitive obedience requires accuracy and precision, make sure you make it fun for your Cocker, with lots of praise and rewards so that you motivate him to do his best. Many training clubs run advanced classes for those who want to compete in obedience, or you can hire the services of a professional trainer so you can have one-on-one sessions.

To be successful in the show ring, a Cocker must conform as closely as possible to the Breed Standard, which is a written blueprint describing the 'perfect' Cocker (see Chapter Seven). To get started you need to buy a puppy that has show potential and then train him to perform in the ring. A Cocker will be expected to stand in show pose, gait for the judge in order to show off his natural movement, and to be examined by the judge. This involves a detailed hands-on examination, so your Cocker must be bombproof when handled by strangers.

Many training clubs hold ringcraft classes, which are run by experienced showgoers. At these classes, you will learn how to handle your Cocker in the ring, and you will also find out about rules, procedures and show ring etiquette.

The best plan is to start off at some small, informal shows where you can practise and learn the tricks of the trade before graduating to bigger shows. It's a long haul starting in the very first puppy class, but the dream is to make your Cocker up into a Show Champion.

AGILITY

This fun sport has grown enormously in popularity over the past few years, and Cocker Spaniels from working lines have proven themselves particularly successful at the sport.

If you fancy having a go at agility with your Cocker Spaniel, make sure you have good control over your dog and keep him slim. Agility is a very physical sport, which demands fitness from both

AGILITY

A fast-moving Cocker can prove his
worth when competing in agility.

Basic training for field work starts at a very early age.

faults are awarded for poles down on the jumps, missed contact points on the A-frame, dog walk and seesaw, and refusals. If a dog takes the wrong course, he is eliminated. The winner is the dog that completes the course in the fastest time with no faults. As you progress up the grades, courses become progressively harder with more twists, turns and changes of direction.

If you want to get involved in agility, you will need to find a club that specialises in the sport (see Appendices). You will not be allowed to start training until your Cocker is 12 months old, and you cannot compete until he is 18 months old. This rule is for the protection of the dog, who may suffer injury if he puts strain on bones and joints while he is still growing.

FIELD TRIALS

This is a sport where the Cocker excels, as it tests his natural working ability. There is now a split between working Cockers and show Cockers, and if you are interested in competing in field trials, you will need a Cocker that is bred from working lines.

In field trials, dogs are trained to work in an entirely natural environment. Nothing is set up, staged or artificial. The dogs may be asked to retrieve shot game from any type of terrain, including swamp, thick undergrowth and from water. They also need to perform blind retrieves, where they are sent out to find shot game when they haven't seen it fall. Dogs are judged on their natural game-finding abilities, their work in the shooting field, and their

dog and handler. A fat Cocker is never going to make it as an agility competitor.

In agility competitions, each dog must complete a set course over a series of obstacles, which include:
- Jumps (upright hurdles and long jump)
- Weaves
- A-frame
- Dog walk
- Seesaw
- Tunnels (collapsible and rigid)
- Tyre

Dogs may compete in two types of class – in jumping classes with jumps, tunnels and weaves, or in agility classes, which have the full set of equipment.

When the dog runs the course,

response to their handler. The two most crucial elements are steadiness and obedience.

Cockers are built for this demanding job, with their waterproof coat, athletic physique and their great swimming ability. The other great plus factor is that Cockers love to work closely with their handlers, so, if you put in the training, you could get to the top levels and even make your Cocker into a field trial Champion.

If you are not aiming for the dizzy heights of making up a field trial Champion, you can test your Cocker Spaniel's working ability with the Gundog Working Certificate, which examines basic hunting and retrieving skills in the field. If a show Champion gains a Gundog Working Certificate, he can become a full Champion.

It takes time, patience and dedication to train a Cocker to the level required for field trials.

FLYBALL

Cocker Spaniels can be easily trained to be flyball competitors, and those from working lines are fast and accurate. Flyball is a team sport; the dogs love it, and it is undoubtedly the nosiest of all the canine sports!

Four dogs are selected to run in a relay race against an opposing team. The dogs are sent out by their handlers to jump four hurdles, catch the ball from the flyball box, and then return over the hurdles. At the top level, this sport is fast and furious, and although it is dominated by Border Collies, reliable Cockers can make a big contribution. This is particularly true in multibreed competitions where the team is made up of four dogs of different breeds, and only one can be a Border Collie or a Working

Sheepdog. Points are awarded to dogs and teams. Annual awards are given to top dogs and top teams, and milestone awards are given out to dogs as they attain points throughout their flyballing careers.

DANCING WITH DOGS

This sport is relatively new, but it is becoming increasingly popular. It is very entertaining to watch, but it is certainly not as simple as it looks. To perform a choreographed routine to music with your Cocker demands a huge amount of training.

Dancing with dogs is divided into two categories: heelwork to music and canine freestyle. In heelwork to music, the dog must work closely with his handler and show a variety of close 'heelwork'

positions. In canine freestyle, the routine can be more flamboyant, with the dog working at a distance from the handler and performing spectacular tricks. Routines are judged on style and presentation, content and accuracy.

SUMMING UP

The Cocker Spaniel is the great all-rounder of the canine world: he is a talented working gundog, a glamorous show dog, and, most important of all, a wonderful companion. He has an outstanding temperament, and he is fun and rewarding to live with. Make sure you keep your half of the bargain: spend time socialising and training your Cocker so that you can be proud to take him anywhere and he will always be a credit to you.

THE PERFECT COCKER

Chapter 7

What is the perfect Cocker Spaniel? The idea of this faultless animal is what breeders of Cocker Spaniels throughout the world are striving to achieve. Every owner of a Cocker Spaniel thinks that their own dog is simply the best – and that is as it should be. Breed devotees are united in their enthusiasm for this active, sporting spaniel that has abundant enthusiasm for life, typified by the ever-wagging tail.

The Cocker is a head breed, and great importance is attached to the proportions of the head and to the appealing Cocker expression. But above all, the Cocker Spaniel is a dog of balance, both when standing and when moving, without exaggeration in any part – the whole being worth more than the sum of its parts.

THE SHOW WORLD
In the world of showing and breeding pedigree dogs, there are three governing bodies that have written and officially approved the Breed Standards. These are the Kennel Club (KC) in the United Kingdom, the Federation Cynologique Internationale (FCI), and the American Kennel Club (AKC). The latest revision of the KC Standard was agreed in 1986. This Standard is also officially recognised in all FCI countries, as the FCI adopts the Standard from the breed's country of origin. The FCI includes the kennel clubs in 83 member countries in the following countries:

- Continental European countries (33 countries)
- South America (Argentina, Brazil, Ecuador, Colombia, Chile, Mexico, Panama, Puerto Rico, Dominican Republic, Uruguay and Venezuela).
- Israel, Morocco, South Korea, Japan, Philippines and Thailand

There are several other countries that are not affiliated with the FCI but are associated with it, namely: Australia, Bermuda, Bolivia, Bulgaria, Cyprus, Gibraltar, Greece, Romania, San Marino, Costa Rica, Cuba, Guatemala, Honduras, Hong Kong, Iceland, India, Indonesia, Ireland, Malta, Malaysia, Madagascar, New Zealand, South Africa and Zimbabwe. In these countries the British Standard is the official Standard.

Similarly, the American Kennel Club has drawn up its own Standards for all pedigree dogs recognised in the United States.

The three governing bodies register pedigree dogs in different groups, depending on each breed's working ancestry. The names of the groups, and some of the breeds included,

The judge uses the Breed Standard as the basis of assessing Cocker Spaniels in the show ring.

may vary, but there are usually only minor differences. In the UK, the Kennel Club has seven groups: the Toy Group, the Working Group, the Pastoral Group, the Utility Group, the Terrier Group, the Hound Group and the Gundog Group.

Cocker Spaniels are included in the Gundog Group (known as the Sporting Group in the USA), along with many other spaniels and retrievers. The spaniels within the group are: the American Cocker Spaniel, the Brittany Spaniel, the Clumber Spaniel, the English Springer Spaniel, the Field Spaniel, the Irish Water Spaniel, the Sussex Spaniel, and the Welsh Springer Spaniel.

A STANDARD OF PERFECTION

Each breed is judged to a Breed Standard – but what exactly is a Breed Standard? It is best described as 'a Standard of perfection'. The Standard is compiled, agreed and controlled by the relevant governing body of pedigree dogs – which is the Kennel Club in the UK. When the Cocker Spaniel Club was founded in 1902, it adopted the Breed Standard as written by the Kennel Club. The original Standard considered each aspect of the dog's formation and movement, and awarded points to each aspect. Thus, the perfect Cocker Spaniel would have been awarded 100 points. For a period of 60 years or more, Cocker Spaniels were judged against this Standard. In 1969, the Cocker Spaniel Club instigated a revision. After discussion with Cocker Spaniel clubs home and abroad, some alterations were made to the Standard. The scale of points was dropped, and changes were made to clarify and remove unnecessary

wording. The changes did not change the appearance of the breed in any way. The main changes that were introduced were:

- Approximate heights of dogs replaced the previous strict limits.
- Before the changes, the Standard stated: "*The neck should be long, strong and muscular, and neatly set on to fine sloping shoulders.*" After revision, the Standard states: "*Necks to be moderate in length, muscular. Set neatly in to fine sloping shoulders.*" Some breeders took this Standard to the extreme and started breeding Cockers with exaggerated necks.

Subsequent to these revisions, the Kennel Club decided to standardise all of its breed descriptions. All breeds now have the same format. These were brought together in the Kennel Club publication of the *Illustrated Breed Standards* in 1986.

It should be remembered that all judges use the Breed Standard as the basis of their assessment. Most Cocker Spaniel enthusiasts will visualise the perfect Cocker in a very similar light, but it is very rare for two people to interpret the Standard in exactly the same way. The perfect Cocker Spaniel as yet remains unborn, although many superb specimens can be seen in the show ring. The Cocker Spaniel is an ancient breed and it marches to perfection as time progresses. The top-winning Cocker Spaniels, often close to perfection, will still be judged and beaten in the show ring by some dogs that are of a lesser type because, in the opinion of the judge, they are not as good. Perhaps they did not move as well, or just did not show as well that day, for example.

To understand the Standard properly, it is necessary to refer to a living specimen whose worth is freely acknowledged in the breed by a number of Championship judges. If possible, the dog should be studied while looking at the Standard. The Breed Standard is a word picture of the perfect specimen, and it forms the basis on which modern Cocker Spaniel breeding has been built. Obviously, it cannot possibly make the same picture in different minds. Assuming that you had never seen a Cocker Spaniel before, would you be able to mould a mental picture just by reading the few sentences of the Breed Standard?

The Cocker Spaniel is balanced in looks and character. This is 1996 Crufts Best in Show winner Sh. Ch. Canigou Cambrai.

DETAILED ANALYSIS

The UK Breed Standard and the FCI Standard are identical in every aspect. Thus when judges are assessing the Cocker Spaniel under the KC rules or the FCI rules, they must work to the same Standard. It is not the Standards that differ, merely the awards that can be given and the process undertaken by the judge to be able to declare the best specimen of the breed.

To make a comparison of the different Breed Standards, the Kennel Club/FCI Breed Standard is reproduced below for each aspect of the dog, along with the American Kennel Club Breed Standard. The first difference to note is that the AKC Standard refers to the English Cocker Spaniel; the breed we know as the American Cocker Spaniel has the title Cocker Spaniel in the States.

Responding to public concern about the health of pure bred dogs, the KC has inserted the following introductory paragraph in all breed Standards:

A Breed Standard is the guideline which describes the ideal characteristics, temperament and appearance of a breed and ensures that the breed is fit for function. Absolute soundness is essential. Breeders and judges should at all times be careful to avoid obvious conditions or exaggerations which would be detrimental in any way to the health, welfare or soundness of this breed. From time to time certain conditions or exaggerations may be considered to have the potential to affect dogs in some breeds adversely, and judges and breeders are requested to refer to the Kennel Club website for details of any such current issues. If a feature or quality is desirable it should only be present in the right measure.

GENERAL APPEARANCE
KC
Merry, sturdy, sporting; well-balanced; compact; measuring approximately same from

Good temperament is the hallmark of the breed.

withers to ground as from withers to root of tail.

AKC
The English Cocker Spaniel is an active, merry sporting dog, standing well up at the withers and compactly built. He is alive with energy; his gait is powerful and frictionless, capable both of covering ground effortlessly and penetrating dense cover to flush and retrieve game.

Let us consider the differences in the two Standards and interpret what the words mean. The general appearance infers that the Cocker's appearance must be pleasing, that it will impress you and attract your attention. His good demeanour, outline, balance, size, and sound, merry action must be in evidence. The one word that is missing from

the AKC Standard here is 'balance', although it does appear in their Standard under Characteristics. However, balance is the keyword for the breed's appearance. The Cocker Spaniel should be balanced in both looks and in character, with no exaggerations whatsoever. The text for the AKC Standard throughout is much wordier, and contrasts greatly with the more concise KC Standard.

The Cocker Spaniel should have a squarely proportioned body, and should measure approximately the same from the top of the shoulder (withers) to the ground as from the withers to the root of the tail. The length of leg and depth of body should appear proportionate to one another. He should not appear long in the back or short in the leg. With the balance needed throughout, the neck should be in correct relationship to the size of the body.

The Cocker Spaniel should give the appearance of being a strong dog in a small frame, with a happy disposition and a proud, regal demeanour. While the Cocker is built on the line of a hunter – sturdy with the stamina to work all day – his appearance when in full coat with feathering is a look that is very glamorous.

CHARACTERISTICS
KC

Merry nature with ever-wagging tail shows a typical bustling movement, particularly when following scent, fearless of heavy cover.

AKC

His enthusiasm in the field and the incessant action of his tail while at work indicate how much he enjoys the hunting for which he was bred. His head is especially characteristic. He is, above all, a dog of balance, both standing and moving, without exaggeration in any part, the whole worth more than the sum of its parts.

TEMPERAMENT
KC

Gentle and affectionate, yet full of life and exuberance.

AKC

The English Cocker is merry and affectionate, of equable disposition, neither sluggish nor hyperactive, a willing worker and a faithful and engaging companion.

The characteristics and temperament are considered by many to be the most attractive features of the Cocker Spaniel. The typical Cocker temperament is friendly, happy and equable. This intelligent dog can be trained for a wide variety of tasks and he is very adaptable. The Cocker Spaniel is known as The Merry Cocker, and his bustling movement can be evident when on the scent, but also when out on an everyday walk. The intelligence of the Cocker can be too much for his own good; some are self-willed and need firm, fair training from an early age.

HEAD AND SKULL
KC

Square muzzle, with distinct stop set midway between tip of nose and occiput. Skull well developed, cleanly chiselled, neither too fine nor too coarse. Cheek bones not prominent. Nose sufficiently wide for acute scenting power.

AKC

General appearance – strong, yet free from coarseness, softly contoured, without sharp angles. Taken as a whole, the parts combine to produce the expression distinctive of the breed. Expression – Soft, melting, yet dignified, alert, and intelligent. Skull – Arched and slightly flattened when seen both from the side and from the front. Viewed in profile, the brow appears not appreciably higher than the back-skull. Viewed from above, the sides of the skull are in planes roughly parallel to those

The Cocker Spaniel has a well-developed skull, with a square-shaped muzzle.

The ears are set on level with the eyes, and extend to the tip of the nose.

of the muzzle. Stop definite, but moderate, and slightly grooved. Muzzle – Equal in length to skull; well cushioned; only as much narrower than the skull as is consistent with a full eye placement; cleanly chiseled under the eyes. Jaws – Strong, capable of carrying game. Nostrils wide for proper development of scenting ability; color black, except in livers and parti-colors of that shade where they will be brown; reds and parti-colors of that shade may be brown, but black is preferred. Lips – Square, but not pendulous or showing prominent flews.

The head is a very important feature of the Cocker Spaniel. When being judged it is generally the first and last thing the judge looks at. The two Standards leave the interpretation of what the perfect Cocker should look like wide open. The KC Standard is looking for balance without any exaggeration in the skull. The AKC Standard gives a lot of detail. The head should have a slightly domed appearance and the skull an oval shape. The stop, which should be distinct, is the point on the head between the eyes, midway between the nose and the occiput.

Heads have varied a great deal over the years in spite of the

Standards. Long, bony skulls, shallow muzzles, and very exaggerated eyebrows are some features that detract from the soft, gentle expression that should be seen. It is worth remembering what Cocker Spaniels were bred for originally when considering the head and skull. The skull should allow for brain room, while the muzzle should be of suitable size and strength to carry game. A term often used when describing a poor head is 'apple headed'. This means that the skull is over-rounded at the top, looking as though there is an apple under the skull. This detracts from the balance of the head, eyes and expression.

EYES
KC
Full, but not prominent. Dark brown or brown, never light, but in the case of liver, liver roan and liver and white, dark hazel to harmonise with coat; with expression of intelligence and gentleness but wide awake, bright and merry; rims tight.

AKC
Acute eyes are essential to the desired expression. They are medium in size, full and slightly oval; set wide apart; lids tight. Haws are inconspicuous; may be pigmented or unpigmented. Eye color dark brown, except in livers and liver parti-colors where hazel is permitted, but the darker the hazel the better.

So much can be learnt from the eyes of a Cocker Spaniel. The expression should be one of

The neck should be long enough to pick up game, and strong enough to carry it for some distance.

frankness and openness, indicating an honest character. A full eye rim is not desirable, as it would be in danger of getting damaged by brambles. A narrow/slitty eye, or an almond-shaped eye, can suggest a sly temperament. Loose skin around the eye gives a hooded appearance and a shifty expression – and it must be difficult for the dog to see properly. Loose eyes means that the rim of the eye is saggy, which is really unsightly, and the eyes are more prone to getting foreign bodies in them. Sometimes the eye will have a white or flesh-coloured third eyelid; this may be confined to one eye, while the other eye has a dark third eyelid. If the rims are not loose, this is not overly disadvantageous to the dog.

Many judges are fanatical about heads and expression when judging, and the colour of the eyes is so important in this aspect. The KC Standard asks for the eye colour to harmonise with the coat. The AKC does not stipulate this and, possibly, leaves the colour open to a wider interpretation. A difficulty can occur with a Cocker who has liver/chocolate colouring; instead of the harmonising hazel eye, a rather yellow or 'gooseberry' eye may be seen. Some breeders will maintain that this is an indication of doubtful temperament.

EARS
KC
Lobular, set low on a level with eyes. Fine leathers extending to nose tip. Well clothed with long, straight silky hair.

AKC
Set low, lying close to the head; leather fine, extending to the nose, well covered with long, silky, straight or slightly wavy hair.

The Standards here are almost identical, except that the AKC does not specify that the ears should be set on a level with the eyes. The design of the ears was to offer protection for a dog working in the field. The Cocker lifts his ears when listening, and often tips his head to one side to make sure he can hear clearly. While the hair on the ears should be long, straight and silky, it should not be excessive, as this often leads to matted or tangled hair.

121

The Cocker is strong and compact, giving the impression of strength and heaviness.

MOUTH
KC
Jaws strong with a perfect, regular and complete scissor bite, i.e. upper teeth closely overlapping lower teeth and set square to the jaws.

AKC
Bite – Scissors. A level bite is not preferred. Overshot or undershot to be severely penalized.

The difference in the Standards is the words "not preferred" in the AKC Standard. This would suggest that a level bite could be acceptable. This is not the case for the KC/FCI Standard. If you listen to breeders talking about Cocker Spaniel mouths, they often say that a dog has a bad mouth. This does not mean that the dog has bad breath or a mouth infection, but that the teeth are not all in the correct position. Thus, one

crooked tooth to some judges is deemed to be a 'bad mouth'. An overshot mouth is one where the upper teeth protrude significantly; an undershot mouth is where the lower teeth extend beyond the upper jaw.

Cocker Spaniels as gundogs also have what is called a 'soft' mouth. This means that they should be able to carry game firmly but gently without damaging it.

NECK
KC
Moderate in length, muscular. Set neatly into fine sloping shoulders. Clean throat.

AKC
Graceful and muscular, arched toward the head and blending cleanly, without throatiness, into sloping shoulders; moderate in length and in balance with the length and height of the dog.

The Standard is asking for a strong neck that is long enough to be able to pick up game and strong enough to carry it some distance, even over fences and through water. Head carriage is important when the Cocker Spaniel is moving, and an adequate length should enable them to move elegantly. To hold the head elegantly there should be an obvious curve from the base of the skull. If this is the case, the head can be held high, and when the nose is pointing down, the lovely dome of the skull can be seen.

In both Standards the terms 'clean throat' or 'without throatiness' are used. Throatiness is referring to any loose or sagging skin hanging underneath the jaw.

Fine, sloping shoulders mean that there should be a small gap between the shoulder blades so that they do not meet or rub when in movement. Too wide a gap would create a front that is too wide. If they are too close and the shoulders are upright, the dog would be too narrow in front. The shoulder blade should be set at a distinct angle, ideally 45 degrees. The lay of the shoulder permits the length of the neck. The more upright (straight) the shoulder blade is, the shorter the neck.

BODY
KC
Strong, compact. Chest well developed and brisket deep; neither too wide nor too narrow in front. Ribs well sprung. Loin short, wide with firm, level topline gently sloping downwards to tail from end of loin to set on of tail.

THE JUDGE'S EXAMINATION

The judge will make an individual examination of every dog in the ring.

All attention is on the dog; the judge should pay no attention to who is handling the dog.

After the examination, the judge will ask the handler to move the dog so he can assess gait and overall conformation.

The judge will select the best Cocker male, and the best Cocker female, from all the classes he has judged.

and lungs of an active dog, a well-developed chest, well-sprung ribs and a deep brisket (the lower part of the body below the chest wall and between the forelegs). Viewed from above, the shape of a Cocker Spaniel is slightly narrower behind the withers, before widening for the ribs to a more or less barrel shape before decreasing to a waistline at the loin.

FOREQUARTERS
KC
Shoulders sloping and fine. Legs well boned, straight, sufficiently short for concentrated power. Not too short to interfere with tremendous exertions expected from this grand, sporting dog.

AKC
The English Cocker is moderately angulated. Shoulders are sloping, the blade flat and smoothly fitting. Shoulder blade and upper arm are approximately equal in length. Upper arm set well back, joining the shoulder with sufficient angulation to place the elbow beneath the highest point of the shoulder blade when the dog is standing naturally.

The limbs of the Cocker Spaniel should be straight and strong to enable them to work all day. The bone should be well rounded and not fine and spindly; this goes back to the purpose of the breed, which needed a strong, small dog that could work in thick undergrowth or move through the heather on the moors.

AKC
Compact and well-knit, giving the impression of strength without heaviness. Chest deep; not so wide as to interfere with action of forelegs, nor so narrow as to allow the front to appear narrow or pinched. Fore chest well developed, prosternum projecting moderately beyond shoulder points. Brisket reaches to the elbow and slopes gradually to a moderate tuck-up. Ribs well sprung and springing gradually to mid-body, tapering to back ribs which are of good depth and extend well back. Back short and strong. Loin short, broad and very slightly arched, but not enough to affect the topline appreciably. Croup gently rounded, without any tendency to fall away sharply.

Tail - Docked. Set on to conform to croup. Ideally, the tail is carried horizontally and is in constant motion while the dog is in action. Under excitement, the dog may carry his tail somewhat higher, but not cocked up. Topline – The line of the neck blends into the shoulder and backline in a smooth curve. The backline slopes very slightly toward a gently rounded croup, and is free from sagging or rumpiness.

The Standards are, again, very different in length, with very much more description in the AKC Standard. It is considered in both Standards that the body should be of a compact appearance, deep and short. The construction must be such as to allow plenty of room for the heart

Traditionally the Cocker was shown with a docked tail.

HINDQUARTERS

KC

Wide, well rounded, very muscular. Legs well boned, good bend of stifle, short below hock allowing for plenty of drive.

AKC

Angulation moderate and, most importantly, in balance with that of the forequarters. Hips relatively broad and well rounded. Upper thighs broad, thick and muscular, providing plenty of propelling power. Second thighs well muscled and approximately equal in length to the upper. Stifle strong and well bent. Hock to pad short. Feet as in front.

It is worth considering the components of the hindquarters.

There are three main sections – the thigh bone, the second thigh, and the stifle joint – each at a distinct angle to the next. The hock is often deemed to be too long or too short, but, in fact, this is not possible, as the hock is a joint. As with all parts of the Cocker Spaniel, balance is the key word in the construction of the hindquarters. If they are exaggerated, the Cocker will become unbalanced. The strong propulsion of movement comes from a well-rounded rear end, well-muscled hind legs, and hocks that stand well apart.

FEET

KC

Firm, thickly padded, cat-like.

AKC

Proportionate in size to the legs, firm, round and catlike; toes arched and tight; pads thick.

The AKC is more specific to actual size of the feet. If the Cocker has well-rounded bone, the feet should appear almost a continuation of the leg. When some feet are trimmed, it is evident that the groomer has not looked at a cat's foot. The feet are trimmed very short between the toes thus making the feet appear flat and wide, quite the opposite from the requirements of the Standard!

TAIL

KC

Set on slightly lower than line of back. Must be merry in action and carried level, never cocked up. Previously customarily docked (*Previously*

The Cocker's gait is characterised by the power and drive he would need for working in dense cover and upland terrain.

recently added to the KC Standard).

Docked: Never too short to hide, nor too long to interfere with, the incessant merry action when working.

Undocked: Slightly curved, of moderate length, proportionate to size of body giving an overall balanced appearance; ideally not reaching below the hock. Strong at the root and tapering to a fine tip; well feathered in keeping with the coat. Lively in action, carried on a plane not higher than level of back and never so low as to indicate timidity.

AKC

Docked. Set on to conform to croup. Ideally, the tail is carried horizontally and is in constant motion while the dog is in action. Under excitement, the dog may carry his tail somewhat higher, but not cocked up.

This is where the Standards will differ, as the new legislation in the United Kingdom bans the docking of tails on any Cocker Spaniels (and all other customarily docked breeds) who are not working dogs. The docking ban has been operative in Scandinavia for some time.

The merry Cocker is evident from an ever-wagging tail, but if it is cocked up or carried high, a rather dominant temperament may be indicated. A tail carried low or tucked underneath indicates an unhappy, shy or timid dog. In the show ring, a Cocker Spaniel that has a 'gay' or proud tail is often penalised, because it is such an obvious fault.

GAIT/MOVEMENT

KC

True through action with great drive covering ground well.

AKC

The English Cocker is capable of hunting in dense cover and upland terrain. His gait is accordingly characterized more by drive and the appearance of power than by great speed. He covers ground effortlessly and with extension both in front and in rear, appropriate to his angulation. In the ring, he carries his head proudly and is able to keep much the same topline while in action as when standing for examination. Going and coming, he moves in a straight line without crabbing or rolling, and with width between both front and rear legs appropriate to his build and gait.

The gait/movement of the Cocker Spaniel should be true and sound throughout. The legs should move straight forward, neither turning in nor out. The legs should not move too close together, neither fore nor aft.

COAT
KC
Flat, silky in texture, never wiry or wavy, not too profuse and never curly. Well feathered forelegs, body and hind legs above hocks.

AKC
On head, short and fine; of medium length on body; flat or slightly wavy; silky in texture. The English Cocker is well-feathered, but not so profusely as to interfere with field work. Trimming is permitted to remove overabundant hair and to enhance the dog's true lines. It should be done so as to appear as natural as possible.

The KC Standard of the Cocker Spaniel states that "the coat should be flat, silky in texture, never wiry, not too profuse and never curly". If only that were the case for all Cocker Spaniels! Many coats have some waves in them and are often very profuse. Some of the heaviest and thickest coats are found in the solid colours

A mismarked Cocker is described as 'unfortunately marked'. This is of no consequence for working dogs or pets.

(black, red or golden). If, however, the coat is groomed regularly and properly, even the thickest coat can be managed. It should be remembered that if a dog is neutered or a bitch spayed, there can be an adverse reaction to the coat. A previously good, smooth, flat coat often becomes much thicker and curlier and difficult to manage. I have found in these instances that careful use of clippers on the coat is the only

way that such a coat can be managed.

It is interesting with this part of the Standard that the AKC refers to the trimming of the coat. The trimming is not mentioned anywhere in the KC/FCI Standard. Perhaps this is why the English Cocker Spaniel shown in the United States is trimmed much more severely and looks much more sculptured than in the UK or on the Continent?

COLOUR
KC
Various. In self colours no white allowed except on chest.

AKC
Various. Parti-colors are either clearly marked, ticked or roaned, the white appearing in combination with black, liver or shades of red. In parti-colors it is preferable that solid markings be broken on the body and more or less evenly distributed; absence of body markings is acceptable. Solid colors are black, liver or shades of red. White feet on a solid are undesirable; a little white on throat is acceptable; but in neither case do these white markings make the dog a parti-color. Tan markings, clearly defined and of rich shade, may appear in conjunction with black, livers and parti-color combinations of those colors. Black and tans and liver and tans are considered solid colors.

Cocker colours have been described fully in Chapter One. The pigmentation of Cocker Spaniels, which is the colour of the nose, pads and eyes, can either be black or brown. The brown pigmentation can be found in the liver or chocolate roan, the orange roan, and the lemon roan. The soles of the feet (pads) on parti-colours are always fully pigmented. They will be completely black in blue roans, orange roans or lemon roans that have black pigmentation, and brown in liver/chocolate, orange and lemon roans that have brown pigmentation. Interestingly, the only exception to this is with newborn puppies, when each foot has a fully pigmented line around the outer edge of the sole on each foot. This will fill in gradually until, at about 10 days of age, the soles will be completely covered.

In Cocker Spaniels, a mismarked dog is not recognised as such, but it is described as being unfortunately marked. If you are buying a pet Cocker, and you have no intentions of showing him, a dog with 'different' markings may even have added novelty value. The dog will certainly make as good a pet as a correctly marked Cocker. However, it is interesting to discover what breeders are aiming to achieve in order to conform with the Breed Standard.

In a well-marked Cocker, the areas of black (or liver/chocolate, orange or lemon) patching will cover the ears, both sides of the skull and around the root of the tail. There may be patches of colour anywhere else over the neck, legs, body and hindquarters. In a Cocker that is unfortunately marked, these markings may be partially or wholly absent, with roaned areas in their place. The head may be solid black, but the most usual form is for a flash or blaze of roan to cover the majority of the muzzle and to run up between the eyes, over the stop, to the back skull. In the darker roans, it would be usual for the head markings on the side of the skull to join over the occiput, with either no spot or the spot isolated from other markings. There is no hard-and-fast rule as to how roan Cocker Spaniels should be marked. In the show ring, uneven or even absence of patching should not be penalised, but anything other than the true head markings may not flatter the appearance of the head and expression. Roaned stripes can often be found inside the ears, but it is very unusual to see a Cocker Spaniel with white ears.

In solid colours, white marking is only allowed on the chest, but it must not be too dominant. Yet with the working Cockers, white markings on the head or tail are valued, as they can be useful for spotting a dog when he is working in bush and undergrowth. There is a greater variation of colours within the working strains, as it is the working skills that are bred for. In the show ring this is not the case and generally solid-colour Cockers are not mated to parti-colours, which prevents the wider range of colours.

SIZE
KC
Height approximately: dogs: 39-41 cms (15.5-16 ins); bitches: 38-39 cms (15-15.5 ins). Weight approximately: 13-14.5 kgs (28-32 lbs).

AKC
Height at withers: males 16 to 17 inches; females 15 to 16 inches. Deviations to be penalized. The most desirable weights: males, 28 to 34 pounds; females, 26 to 32 pounds. Proper conformation and substance should be considered more important than weight alone. Proportion - Compactly built and short-coupled, with height at withers slightly greater than the distance from withers to set-on of tail. Substance - The English Cocker is a solidly built dog with as much bone and

substance as is possible without becoming cloddy or coarse.

It is within the sizes that the most obvious differences in the Standards can be found. A Cocker in the USA is allowed to be up to a full inch (2.5 cm) taller and two pounds (0.9 kg) heavier than a male dog under KC/FCI Standards. Bitches have a size difference of half an inch (1.25 cm) and a weight difference up to two pounds (0.9 kg). The height of a Cocker Spaniel is measured from the top of the shoulder blade (withers) to the ground.

FAULTS
KC
Any departure from the foregoing points should be considered a fault and the seriousness with which the fault should be regarded should be in exact proportion to its degree, *and its effect upon the health and welfare of the dog, and the dog's ability to perform its traditional work* (this highlighted phrase recently added to the KC Standard).
Note: Male animals should have two apparently normal testicles fully descended into the scrotum.

It is interesting that the Standard from the American Kennel Club does not give any faults for the Cocker Spaniel. Their Standard is much more detailed and assumes that if all the Standards are met, the perfect Cocker Spaniel has been achieved.

PRESENTATION
The presentation of the Cocker Spaniel in the show ring can make the perfect Cocker or near-perfect Cocker appear to look terrible. A skilled groomer can manage to accentuate the positive points of the dog and cleverly hide the more negative aspects of the construction. To many of the older expert breeders, presentation means the whole condition of the Cocker Spaniel, not just its coat. A Cocker Spaniel that is well muscled, in good coat, and with plenty of substance and body, is considered to be well presented. This type of dog, if made properly, will move to show off his virtues to advantage. Many newer exhibitors consider that the presentation is just how the coat looks after careful and clever trimming. But beauty should not be considered to be skin deep.

It should also be remembered that the handling of the dog in the ring can make the most out of an average specimen, or make a good dog look poor. Training a new puppy for the ring is advantageous from an early age. If both the handler and the dog know what to do, then the well-constructed, well-behaved, and expertly presented Cocker Spaniel must be very close to the perfect Cocker. However, at the end of the day, everyone who owns a Cocker Spaniel has the perfect Cocker. The Standards are there to help breeders achieve perfection, but whether we work, show or just enjoy the company of a pet dog, your own Cocker Spaniel should be the one that you always want to take home.

Win or lose, the Cocker Spaniel you take home is the most perfect dog for you.

HAPPY AND HEALTHY

Chapter 8

The temperament of the Cocker Spaniel is alert and happy; he thrives on human company and is always ready to join in with family activities. A dog's life is more fulfilled when he has opportunities for exercise and can use his eyes and nose to stimulate his interest in activities. As a working dog, the Cocker has proved his ability in scenting and retrieving game, and has now shown himself to be adept in scenting out many diverse substances, such as explosives and illegal substances.

In order to keep your Cocker healthy, there must be opportunities for interesting walks to provide exercise; he must be fed a balanced diet to maintain a fit body; and he needs veterinary care with necessary vaccinations and parasite control. Visits to the veterinary surgeon are required for vaccinations, at which time it is usual to make a physical examination of the dog for any undisclosed disease. In between times, daily grooming provides the opportunity to get to know the dog's coat and the body structure, so that signs of illness can be detected earlier than if left until the dog is in pain or refusing his food. Improved diet and routine vaccinations are contributing to a much longer life for all domestic animals, but the carer of the dog has a role to play in everyday health care. It is very important that you really get to know your dog, as you will more easily identify when the dog is not right or is 'off colour' and seek appropriate veterinary advice.

VACCINATIONS

One of the greatest advances in canine practice in the last 50 years has been the development of effective vaccines to prevent diseases. Within living memory dogs died with fits, after distemper virus infections, and in the last 20 years many puppies have had parvovirus, which resulted in many fatalities until a vaccine was developed. The routine use of a multiple component vaccine to protect against canine distemper, infectious canine hepatitis, parvovirus and leptospirosis is accepted, but there are still local differences in the age the puppy receives his first injection or 'shot'.

The timing for the primary vaccine course is based on an understanding of when the immunity, provided by the mother, declines to a level that will not interfere with the pup's immune response. Canine vaccines currently in use have recommendations for the final dose of the primary course to be given at 10 or 12 weeks of age; and boosters after the first year are usual. With the working breeds, this annual dose is especially necessary for protection against potentially fatal

Vaccination prevents the spread of infectious diseases among dogs.

Leptospirosis, which occurs in water and where rats have been present. The length of protection provided after two injections for the puppy is not significantly greater than 12 months (challenges after this date results in shedding of Leptospires), and for some vaccines it is even considered less than 12 months. For protection against the other viruses, a minimum of three years is possible, and annual boosters are less essential. However, further booster vaccination is recommended at intervals, decided by the vet who has local knowledge of disease incidence. This will protect dogs that may have low or marginal blood level titres.

Kennel cough is a distressing infectious disease usually acquired from airborne contact with other dogs, especially those stressed when visiting dog shows or boarding kennels. There are several vaccines available, and, again, advice should be obtained from the vet as to which type of protection is appropriate to the dog's exposure.

Rabies vaccine is necessary for all dogs leaving the United Kingdom, but is routine in many countries, as is the vaccine for Lyme disease in the US, where protection policy should be discussed with a veterinarian. (See Ailments A-Z for more information on these infectious diseases.)

WORMING AND PARASITE CONTROL

Routine worming every three months is obligatory to reduce the risk of infection of susceptible humans handling the dog. De-wormers are necessary for puppies as well as for adult dogs. Many puppies are infested with roundworms, but some breeders will start worming the pregnant bitch to reduce the risk to the newborn pups. Worming of a puppy from two weeks, repeated at regular intervals, is advised. Roundworms, hookworms, tapeworms and whipworms present different threats, while heartworms, which can result from the bite of an infected mosquito, are a particular problem of the south-east Atlantic and Gulf Coasts of the USA, and with climate change has become an increasing threat in the UK. Those dog owners planning to take their pet to mainland Europe should know that heartworm is endemic for the Mediterranean area of France, but, with global warming, is slowly spreading northwards.

A single flea on the dog's coat can cause persistent scratching and restlessness. Many effective anti-flea preparations are now available; some as tablets by mouth, some as coat applications, and some as residual sprays to apply to carpets and upholstery frequented by cats as well as dogs. Your own vet will advise you of the best product for your dog.

Lice, fleas, Cheyletiella, those mites that burrow under the skin and the mites on the surface, may all cause disease and are not always recognised. The exception are ticks that become large and visible as they gorge themselves with the dog's blood. A thorough grooming of the dog each day will detect many of these parasites, and suitable preventive products should be applied as needed. These may be supplied as a powder, a shampoo, a spot-on insecticide, or a spray.

DIET AND EXERCISE FOR HEALTH

Some Cockers are naturally lean, and although they look as though they are underweight they are perfectly fit, even though they appear to carry little body fat. More sedentary Cockers may be inclined to put on weight as they get older. It is a good idea to weigh dogs on a regular basis; the dog that appears thin but still actively fit has fewer reserves to fall back on, and weighing on a weekly basis can detect further weight loss before any disastrous change can occur. Each dog should have an ideal weight and, within a narrow range, the actual correct weight for the dog will act as a guide. Obesity has become a major concern for dogs as well as humans, and appetite suppressants for dogs, prescribed by your vet, can now be used as part of an overall weight management programme.

COAT, EARS AND FEET

The Cocker's coat should be quite dense and waterproof. Too much confinement indoors, with warm room temperatures, can lead to loss of the undercoat and less hair density for outdoor protection. Regular brushing and grooming helps to stimulate the skin and provides an opportunity for close inspection of the underlying skin:

- Grooming stimulates the hair growth stage known as anagen by the removal of dead, shedding hairs. This helps to prevent bareness or bald patches.

- The removal of eye discharge, or other form of discharge, prevents coat matting and prevents skin irritation.

Spot-on treatment is effective in the battle against fleas.

AILMENTS A-Z

ALLERGIES

Allergies are now a common diagnosis for many dogs with skin or intestinal disorders. The condition results from an inappropriate immune response by the dog to an antigen substance, either in the food or inhaled through the nose. A process of eliminating possible antigens in the diet or in the environment, may help to find a cause – and there are commercial diets available that may help.

Medication can be used to suppress the allergic response and both antihistamines and steroids may be tried before the most suitable treatment is found.

ANAL DISORDERS

Modern diets are often blamed for the high incidence of dogs needing their anal 'glands'

squeezed out at regular intervals. These glands are actually little sacs just at the edge of the anus opening, and they contain strong-smelling, greasy substances used to 'mark' the freshly passed faeces for other animals to recognise.

Over-production of the fluid causes the dog discomfort, and, when a suitable floor surface is available, the dog will then 'scoot' along, leaving a trail of odorous matter. Occasionally, infection of the gland will alter the smell, and this may result in other dogs being attracted to a female-type odour. A course of antibiotics can have a direct benefit on this apparent behaviour problem.

Abscesses of the anal sacs are very painful; they may require drainage although often they swell and burst on their own with a sudden blood-stained discharge. Flushing out and antibiotics may be required as treatment.

Other glands around the anus may become cancerous, and attention is drawn to these if bleeding occurs. Adenomata are tumours found in the older male dog and require veterinary attention before bleeding occurs.

ARTHRITIS

This joint disease is found after an infection, but now the condition is usually either due to joint wear and tear (degenerative), or as a result of an immune system reaction – rheumatoid arthritis and

GROOMING CHECKLIST

Close inspection of the animal during grooming assists in the early recognition of problems. The ears need daily attention to spot signs of staining or discharge. The start of ear trouble can be detected by observing the way that the dog holds his head and the use of your nose to smell out trouble!

During grooming, pay attention to any bony prominences or skin folds. Lip folds too should be checked for saliva soaking or unpleasant breath smells. Check for traces of fleas or ticks to prevent itching and hair loss. Some of the spaniel breeds are more prone to labial eczema than other working breeds. Bathing may be needed either to eradicate and control ectoparasites, or to cleanse the coat and remove smells, as well as for cosmetic reasons, such as improving a dog's appearance before a show.

The pads of the feet should feel quite soft to touch and not leathery or horny (hyperkeratinised). The pigment of the foot pads is often similar to the nose colour. Between the toes is an area of skin that is hairy and contains sebaceous glands used for scent marking. Occasionally, cysts and swellings develop if the glands become blocked. The skin between the toes is very sensitive to chemical burns, and some alkaline clay soils will provoke inflammation with lameness known as 'pedal eczema'. Warts are sometimes found on the feet of young dogs, especially those kept in kennels, as feet can become too wet if the dogs are kept on concrete runs that are regularly washed.

The nails should be of even length and not split at the ends after being left to grow too long. If the nails are too long, they need to be clipped, taking care to avoid hurting the dog by cutting into the quick. Exercise on hard, concrete surfaces is normally sufficient to keep nails at a reasonable length; tarmac roads and tarred pavements do not provide enough friction to wear down nails. Dewclaws, if present, are not a disadvantage to the dog. But they will need to be trimmed if they grow in a circle, as they can penetrate the flesh, causing an infected wound.

idiopathic arthritis being examples.

At first, degenerative arthritis improves with exercise, but afterwards the dog will stiffen, and, on bending the joint, often a painful grating 'crepitus' can be found. Treatment will be aimed at keeping the dog mobile, excess weight should be lost, and anti-inflammatory medication on a daily basis will remove pain and discomfort.

Blood tests and X-rays may be needed for investigating arthritis. Some owners have good results with supplements, such as the glycosaminoglycans. For the Cocker's comfort, provide soft, comfortable bedding and encourage frequent short walks

ATOPY

Sometimes known as inhalant allergy, atopy is associated with many chronic skin diseases characterised by pruritus – a sensation within the skin that provokes the Cocker to have a desire to scratch, lick, chew or rub itself to alleviate the irritation. Not as common as in some other breeds, it may require specific tests and medication to relieve the itching.

The signs do not usually develop until one to three years. The characteristic roughened, itchy, oozing skin may be caused by the immune reactions to various allergens, such as fleas or pollen. There is an indication of an inherited tendency, and there is often a seasonal change if specific pollens are the cause.

Seborrhoea may be found as a greasy or excessive scaly skin in some Cockers; it is thought to be partially inherited and partially caused by allergy.

AURAL HAEMATOMA
This is where the ear flap sudden swells due to internal bleeding between the skin and the ear cartilage. It can be distressing to a Cocker and will cause repeated head shaking. Bleeding is usually the result of fierce scratching with the hind toes, perhaps triggered by a tingling inside the ear canal.

Grass seeds or other foreign bodies entering the tube of the outer ear will also provoke such scratching. Ear mites, acquired from cats, can have a similar effect.

When haematoma occur in Cocker Spaniels, treatment usually involves draining the blood under general anaesthesia and implementing measures to stop the dog shaking his head, thus preventing further bleeding. See also Otitis externa.

BRONCHITIS
Inflammation of the breathing tubes is often the result of a virus or a bacterial infection, but irritant gases and dust can also be the cause of repeated coughing. Kennel cough is the most common infection, which results in sticky mucus clinging to the base of the windpipe (trachea) and the tubes entering the lungs (bronchii). Coughing similar to bronchitis is seen in older dogs associated with congestive heart failure, which may occur with a failing heart muscle and fluid accumulating in the lungs.

Antibiotics may be prescribed by the vet to reduce the bronchitis signs, and the risk of further bacterial infection leading to generalised pneumonia. Cough suppressants and 'antitussives' can be used to suppress a persistent cough, but should not be used if there is bronchopneumonia. Steam inhalations, often with a volatile oil, have been used to relieve a dry cough in Cockers.

BURNS AND SCALDS
First-aid measures for burns and scalds require immediate cooling of the skin, which can be done by pouring cold water over the affected part repeatedly for at least 10 minutes. Some scalds, where hot water or oil have been spilt, penetrate the coat. They may not be recognised until a large area of skin and hair peels away, after heat has killed the surface skin cells.

As these injuries are considered to be very painful, analgesics (pain relief) should be obtained and in anything but the smallest injured area, antibiotics would be advised, as secondary bacteria will multiply on exposed raw surfaces. Bandages and dressings are not a great help, but clingfilm has been used in some situations. Clipping

Cockers are generally a healthy breed, but it is important to be aware of common canine ailments.

the hair away over a large area surrounding the burn, then flushing the areas with saline may be tolerated by the dog.

An Elizabethan collar may be used to prevent the Cocker licking the area. In cases showing signs of shock, intravenous fluid therapy may be a necessity.

CALCULI (BLADDER STONES)

Stones were often thought to be the cause of straining to pass urine, and where these signs are shown a veterinary examination for bladder inflammation (cystitis) or tumours is advised.

Calculi are deposits of mineral salts from the urine, either in the neck of the bladder or nearer the base of the penis in the male.

Stones can also form in the kidneys and these cause pain as they enter the ureters; the bladder is not affected.

Calculi are recognisable on X-ray or with ultrasound examinations. The obstruction may be partial when the dog or bitch spends an unusually long time passing urine, or, more frequently in males, no urine can be voided. The dog will strain, looking uncomfortable or in pain.

An operation is usually needed to remove calculi, and dietary advice will be given on how to avoid further attacks. Increasing the dog's water intake and providing opportunities for frequent bladder emptying are equally important in prevention.

CANCER – CARCINOMA

The frequency of cancer in Cockers is no greater than in any other breed, but as dogs are now living longer, owners are more likely to be faced with a cancer diagnosis, particularly in the dog's later years. One in every four dogs will have one of the many types of cancer.

CATARACTS

(See Inherited disorders)

CONSTIPATION

Unless the Cocker is known to have consumed large quantities of bone or fibrous matter, straining may well be due to an enlarged prostate gland in the male, or any foreign body in the rectum. Increasing the fluid intake and the medication of liquid paraffin is advised, but if the problem persists, the vet should be consulted.

CYSTITIS

Inflammation of the bladder is more common in the bitch, and may first be noticed when the animal strains frequently, passing only small quantities of urine. Bladder calculi are fairly common in both sexes and will cause cystitis, but bacteria reaching the bladder from outside the body are the usual cause.

In all cases the fluid intake should be reviewed since a good 'wash through' of the bladder will reduce the risk of bacteria and mineral particles irritating the bladder lining. Medication with antispasmodics and an appropriate antibiotic will be required.

A fit dog that gets plenty of exercise is more likely to lead a long and healthy life.

DIABETES

Dogs suffer from two types of diabetes, but the more common is 'sugar diabetes', known as DM (diabetes mellitus), and is seen more frequently in the older bitch. It is caused by a lack of insulin to regulate the level of glucose in the blood.

The signs of increased thirst, passing large quantities of urine, eye cataracts and muscle weakness are associated with increased appetite and weight loss as the dog attempts to satisfy the variations of its sugar levels.

Diagnosis by urine and blood samples is followed by the injection of a suitable insulin subcutaneously once or more daily. Some types of endocrine disease such as diabetes may arise as a result of an immune-mediated destruction of glandular tissues.

Diabetes insipidus is uncommon in dogs and is related to the water control mechanism of the kidneys.

DISTEMPER

Fortunately, distemper is now a rare virus infection, but at one time it caused devastating illnesses. Routine vaccination has been very effective in preventing disease, but there is always the threat of a Cocker acquiring the infection if there has been a breakdown in the immune system.

Affected dogs develop a high temperature, cough, diarrhoea and a purulent eye discharge. After several weeks, illness complications may still set in with pneumonia or damage to the

The Cocker's long, feathered ears are one of the attractions of the breed, but you need to keep a close check on them to ensure they are clean and healthy.

nervous system shown as nerve twitchings, paralysis or fits.

EPILEPSY AND FITS

Seizures occur relatively commonly in dogs and represent an acute, and usually brief, disturbance of normal electrical activity in the brain. However, it is distressing for both the patient and the owner. Most fits last only a short time (less than two minutes), and owners often telephone for veterinary advice once the seizure is over. Fits can sometimes occur close together.

Following a fit, the dog should be examined by a veterinary surgeon as soon as practical, even if the seizure has stopped. Some fits are prolonged or very frequent; such seizures may cause permanent brain damage. Once

the fits have passed off, the dog may seem dull or confused for several hours. Medication is used to control fits, but long-term treatment may be needed.

EYE PROBLEMS

Conjunctivitis is common in Cocker Spaniels and other breeds that go out in grass. The signs of a red eye with a watery or crusty discharge are easy to recognise. Chemicals and allergies cause irritation, but a presentation of acute, severe conjunctivitis may indicate the presence of a foreign body, such as a grass seed under the eyelids. Careful examination of the inner surfaces of both eyelids, and the third eyelid, is necessary to identify and remove foreign material. Another cause of conjunctivitis is the inturning of

Swimming is an excellent form of exercise, but make sure the conditions are safe before allowing your Cocker to take the plunge.

the edge of the eyelid, known as entropion (see Inherited disorders).

There are other eye disorders, such as corneal ulcers, keratitis and 'dry eye' (KCS), that require specific veterinary attention.

FRACTURES

Most broken bones are the result of injury. An old dog with kidney disease may have brittle bones but spontaneous fractures are quite rare. Treatment of fractures will require the attention of the vet; there is little point in attempting first aid, as the Cocker will be in pain and will adopt the most comfortable position he can find. Natural painkillers, known as endorphins, come into action immediately following such an injury.

If there is a skin wound associated with the fracture, it should be covered to reduce bacterial contamination, thus reducing the risk of osteomyelitis before the break in the bone can be satisfactorily repaired. X-rays will be necessary to confirm a crack or a major displacement of bones.

GASTRO-ENTERITIS

Vomiting is relatively common in dogs, and it can be a protective mechanism to prevent poisonous substances entering the body. Gastro-enteritis includes diarrhoea attacks, which is a similar process of getting rid of undesirable intestine contents by washing them out. The production of extra mucus and intestinal fluid is seen with a rapid bowel evacuation movement. Both products of gastro-enteritis are objectionable:

distressing to the dog and unpleasant for the owner who may have to clean up afterwards. There are many causes, ranging from the simplest of the dog needing worming, to the complex interaction of viruses and bacteria that can cause an infection to spread through a kennel of dogs. A dietary diarrhoea may occur after any sudden change in diet, or it may be caused by scavenging (as when a packet of butter is stolen), or allergy to a particular food substance or an additive. Where the signs of gastro-enteritis last more than 48 hours, a vet should be prepared to take samples and other tests to look for diseases, such as pancreatitis, colitis or tumours, among many other possible causes, since some disorders may be life-threatening.

Treatment at home may be tried

using the principle of 'bowel rest', stopping feeding for 48-72 hours, and allowing fluids in repeated, small quantities. Ice cubes in place of water in the bowl may help reduce vomiting. Electrolyte solutions will help with rehydration. Once signs are alleviated, small feeds of smooth foods, such as steamed fish or chicken, with boiled rice, may be gradually introduced. Where there is continual diarrhoea for three to four weeks, the disease is unlikely to resolve without identifying a specific cause and using appropriate treatment.

GLAUCOMA

Primary glaucoma is an inherited disorder in the Cocker Spaniel, and secondary glaucoma is the term used after some eye injury, or a dislocated lens. The glaucomatous eye becomes more prominent, as there is a rise of fluid pressure within the eyeball due to inadequate drainage of the fluid in the eye globe. This affects the retina and vision fails and may result in permanent blindness. Pain is associated with glaucoma and urgent treatment is needed if the eye has sustained any injury.

HEART AND CARDIAC DISORDERS

Heart disease may show itself in many forms. Young puppies may have abnormal heart sounds and have a congenital heart defect, but cardiac problems are most common in the slightly older Cocker. Reduced exercise and weight increase in the older dog are contributory factors to a failing heart. Medication has improved tremendously in recent years and can give a good long-term prognosis.

There are many conditions of the heart valves and blood vessels that cannot be described here, but weakening of the heart muscle known as myocardial degeneration will often develop. Dilated cardiac myopathy (DCM) is a heart disease found in Cocker Spaniels. Prompt diagnosis by the vet is important since many dogs die within a year, despite treatment. Syncope is the condition reached when the dog collapses; emergency treatment with oxygen and ensured cage rest will be accompanied by appropriate heart medication.

The older Cocker may suffer with mild to severe heart problems, but careful control of exercise and diet can do much to maintain a comfortable old age. One of the common forms is congestive heart failure, seen as a shortness of breath and body

Cocker Spaniels that get sufficient exercise areless prone to obesity and heart disease.

swellings due to retention of sodium and water. Supplements to help the heart muscle may be used; carnitine, arginine and taurine help together with the restriction of dietary sodium. A lowering of salt intake should take place over five days, allowing time for the kidneys to adjust. Some dogs lose their appetite and weight loss results. Special diets containing easily digested energy food and fat to increase palatability may be used.

HEARTWORM DISEASE
Heartworms are becoming more common in the UK but are a major problem in the USA where they are spread by mosquitoes. Dogs may be protected from six to eight weeks of age with a monthly dose of the medication advised by the veterinarian.

There are a number of products available. A blood test can be used to see if the heartworm antigen is present before commencing treatment and it can be repeated annually. The filarial worms live in the heart and blood vessels of the lungs and cause signs such as tiring, intolerance of exercise and a soft, deep cough.

HEPATITIS
Inflammation of the liver may be due to a virus, but it is

LYME DISEASE BORRELIOSIS

The tick-borne disease affecting dogs, humans, and, to a lesser extent, other domestic animals is common in the USA; it is estimated that there may be a thousand cases a year in the UK. Often, it is seen as a sudden lameness with a fever or, in the chronic form, one or two joints are affected with arthritis. Often, lameness in the carpus (wrist joint) alerts the Cocker owner to this disease.

Exposure to ticks (*Ixodes ricinus* in Britain) should raise suspicions if similar signs develop, especially if a rash appears around the bite and quickly spreads. Treatment is effective; blood tests can be used to confirm Borrelia at the laboratory.

uncommon in dogs that have been protected with vaccines that also prevent the bacteria Leptospira damaging the liver.

Chronic liver disease may be due to heart failure, tumours or some type of toxicity: dietary treatment may help if there are no specific medicines to use. The skin condition known as hepato-cutaneous syndrome seems slightly more common in spaniel breeds; it may affect the feet with non-healing sores.

INTERVERTEBRAL DISC DISEASE AND PARALYSIS
Collapse or sudden weakness of the hindquarters may be due to pressure on the nerves of the

spine that supply the muscles and other sensory receptors. The 'slipped disc', as it is commonly known, may be responsible, but any injury to the spine, a fibro cartilage embolism, a fracture or a tumour may cause similar paralysis.

The signs are similar with dragging one or both hind legs, lack of tail use and often the loss of bladder and bowel control. X-rays, a neurological assessment and possibly an MRI scan will be needed to be certain of the cause. Some cases respond well to surgical correction but others will receive medical treatment, which may be effective and is less costly. Home nursing care should keep the dog clean and groomed, help with bladder or bowel movement, and carry out any physiotherapy advised by the veterinary surgeon. Sudden movements in the case of spinal fractures must be avoided, as when carrying a patient with a back injury.

KENNEL COUGH
The signs of a goose-honking cough, hacking or retching that lasts for days to several weeks is due to damage at the base of the windpipe and bronchial tubes. The dry and unproductive cough is caused by a combination of viruses, bacteria and Mycoplasma. Vaccination is helpful in preventing the disease but may

Lyme disease is more likely to affect dogs living in the country.

not give full protection, as strains of kennel cough seem to vary. The disease is highly contagious and spread by droplets, so it may be acquired at dog shows or boarding kennels. An incubation period of five to seven days is usual. Veterinary treatments alleviate the cough and reduce the duration of the illness.

MANGE MITES

Several types of mange mites affect dogs and may be the cause of scratching, hair loss and ear disease. Sarcoptic mange causes the most irritation and is diagnosed by skin scrapings or a blood test.

Demodectic mange is less of a problem and is diagnosed by skin scrapes or from plucked hairs. Otodectic mange occurs in the ears and the mite can be found in the wax. Cheyletiella is a surface mite of the coat; it causes white 'dandruff' signs and is diagnosed by coat brushing or sellotape impressions for microscope inspection.

These mite infections first need identifying, but can then be treated with acaracide medication, such as amitraz, selamectin or imidacloprid and moxidectin, provided by the vet. Repeat treatments after 10 to 14 days are needed to prevent reinfestation.

NEPHRITIS

Dogs may suffer acute kidney failure after poisoning, obstructions to the bladder, or after shock with reduced blood supply. Chronic nephritis is more common in older dogs where the blood accumulates waste products that the damaged kidneys cannot remove. The nephritic syndrome is caused by an immune-mediated damage within the kidney. The signs of increased thirst, loss of appetite and progressive weight loss are commonly seen in kidney disease.

Treatment of chronic renal failure is not reversible, but it aims to reduce the load on the remaining filter units (nephrons) and prevent further damage. Fluid

intake should be encouraged; if the dog is vomiting, intravenous drips will be needed to provide the liquid to help the kidneys work. Taking the dog outside frequently to help bladder emptying is helpful, too. The vet may advise a special diet, and will probably take repeated blood samples to monitor the kidneys' workload.

If the Cocker does not eat, he will start drawing on his own body protein and the condition known as azotaemia will result with severe consequences. A diet of high biological value protein, low in phosphate but rich in vitamin B, will be advised. Diuretics to produce more urine may be used in the nephritic syndrome cases.

OTITIS EXTERNA

Ear diseases are more common in dogs such as the Cocker that have hanging-down ear flaps. When there is a lot of hair around the ear, the ventilation of the tube to the eardrum is poor and may encourage bacteria to multiply. When otitis occurs, a strong-smelling discharge develops and the dog shakes his head or may show a head tilt. Repeated scratching and head shaking may cause a blood haematoma, as a swelling underneath the skin of the ear flap. The presence of a grass seed in the ear canal should always be suspected in Cockers that have been out in long grass in the summer months. After becoming trapped by the hair, the seed can quickly work its way down the ear canal and can even penetrate the eardrum. The spikes of the grass seed prevent it being shaken out of the ear and veterinary extraction of the seed is essential.

PARVOVIRUS

The virus that infects younger dogs is most dangerous to the recently weaned puppy. Vaccination schedules are devised to protect susceptible dogs, and a vet's advice should be asked as to when, and how often, a parvo vaccine should be used in a particular locality.

The virus has an incubation of about three to five days and attacks the bowels with a sudden onset of vomiting and diarrhoea. Blood may be passed, dehydration sets in and sudden death is possible. Isolation from other

LEPTOSPIROSIS

Dogs that live in the country or swim in water may be more prone to this infection. Leptospira bacteria carried by rats may be found in pools and ditches where rodents may have visited. Annual vaccination against the two types of Leptospira is advised.

Treatment in the early stages using antibiotics is effective, but liver and kidney damage may permanently incapacitate the Cocker Spaniel if the early signs, with a fever, are not recognised. Kidney and liver failure will lead to death. Treatment with antibiotics for two to three weeks is needed to prevent the dog carrying Leptospira and infecting others.

puppies is essential; the replacement of the fluids and electrolytes lost is urgent.

Medication to stop the vomiting, antibiotics against secondary bacteria and, later, a smooth, bland diet may be provided.

PROSTATE DISEASE

Elderly Cocker males that have not been castrated may show signs of straining, which may be thought to be a sign of constipation, but an enlarged prostate gland at the neck of the bladder will often be the real cause.

Most often it is a benign enlargement that causes pressure into the rectum, rather than blocking the bladder exit. Once

diagnosed, hormone injections combined with a laxative diet may be very effective.

PYODERMA

A term used by some vets for a bacterial skin infection, it is a condition seen in Cocker Spaniels often associated with wet, oozing skin known as 'wet eczema'.

Treatment should be given to prevent licking and scratching, clipping away hair to encourage a dry surface where bacteria cannot multiply so readily; an appropriate antibiotic can be used. If the bacteria tunnel inwards, it results in the furunculosis skin disorder, which is more difficult to treat.

PYOMETRA

At one time, pyometra was the commonest cause of illness in middle-aged to elderly bitches. This disease of the uterus would be seen in both those bitches never bred from and those who had had litters born earlier in life.

The cause is a hormone imbalance that prepares the lining of the uterus for puppies, but fluid and mucus accumulates, leading to an acute illness if bacteria invade the organ. Known as 'open pyometra' when a blood-stained mucoid discharge comes out, often sticking to the hairs around the vulva, it has been confused with a bitch coming on heat unexpectedly.

It can be more difficult to

diagnose the cause of illness when there is no discharge present, known as 'closed pyometra', and other ways of testing the patient for the uterus disorder may be employed by the vet. Although medical treatments are available it is more usual to perform a hysterectomy, especially if the bitch has come to the end of her breeding career.

RABIES

The fatal virus infection is almost unknown in the UK, but it remains as a cause of death of animals and some humans in parts of the world where preventive vaccine is not in regular use.

The disease attacks a dog's central nervous system; it is spread by infective saliva usually following the bite of an animal developing the disease. Annual rabies vaccination is an important way of controlling the disease.

RINGWORM

This is a fungus disease of the skin that has nothing to do with worms, but it acquired the name from the circular red marks on the skin following infection. It may appear as bald, scaly patches and will spread to children or adults handling the dog unless precautions are taken. Treatments will vary depending on the extent of the problem.

VESTIBULAR DISEASE

Older Cockers may be subject to a condition of a head tilt, often with eye-flicking movements, known as nystagmus. At one time it was commonly diagnosed as a 'stroke' because of its sudden onset. The

dog may circle or fall on one side, and then roll, unable to balance himself.

Vestibular disease develops suddenly but, unlike the equivalent human stroke, there is no sign of bleeding, nor of a vascular accident in the brain. Recovery may take place slowly as the balance centre of the brain regains its use after one to three weeks.

Treatment by the vet will assist a return to normal, although some dogs always carry their head with a tilt.

INHERITED DISORDERS

Genetic diseases have been with us a long time, but improvement of veterinary diagnostic methods and the increased longevity of dogs make it more likely that degenerative diseases will show themselves. Healthy breeding stock should always be selected.

COCKER SPANIEL GLOMERULONEPHROPATHY

This is a form of kidney disease, caused by a recessive gene, which affects dogs of less than two years of age.

This was a problem in the breed, and although occurrence is now rare, there is always the possibility that it might appear in a litter of puppies.

EYE CONDITIONS

Abnormalities of the eyelids may be seen in the young, growing Cocker. A condition known as entropion is where the edge of the eyelid rolls inwards and the lashes rub on the eyeball surface (the

Young puppies that have recently been weaned are vulnerable to parvovirus.

cornea), causing intense irritation and eye watering. Distchiasis and ectopic cilia are other of several eyelid problems of hereditary origins, but such diseases are amenable to surgery.

Conditions that affect the inside of the eye are more serious and can lead to blindness; the retina is the most important site of disease in the eye. Of particular importance is a group of inherited diseases known as progressive retinal atrophy (PRA), which are known to occur in certain families. Folding of the retina, known as retinal dysplasia (RD) is seen from time to time in Cockers; large areas of detachment of the retina will cause blindness.

Cataracts refer to the opacification of the fibres or capsule of the eye lens, ultimately resulting in blindness. A cataract may be present from birth but in the older dog must be distinguished from ageing changes that result in an apparent blue colour of the lens, but through which the animal can still see.

Cataracts may be left untreated or they can be surgically removed by specialist ophthalmic surgeons.

HIP DYSPLASIA

As an inherited disease in many dogs, the breed average score for Cockers is at the level of many other working breeds. The basis of the control scheme is X-ray examination of young adult Cockers in order to identify early signs of hip structure malformation.

Radiographs are taken by the client's own veterinary surgeon after the dog is 12 months old and the photo is submitted for independent 'scoring' under the BVA/Kennel Club scheme (or OFA in the States).

Hip dysplasia disease is a malformation of both the femoral head and acetabulum 'cup' of the hip, which results in lameness, pain and eventual arthritic changes.

Surgical treatments to correct a hip abnormality are used but many cases can be controlled through regular exercise, muscle building, and the use of NSAIDs (non-steroidal, anti-inflammatory drugs).

Anyone buying a puppy should enquire about the hip scores of the parents before completing the purchase.

COMPLEMENTARY THERAPIES

There are many treatments that can be given to dogs over and above the type of medical or surgical treatment that you might have expected by attending a veterinary surgery. Some of these alternative treatments have proved to benefit dogs, while others are better known for their use in humans where the placebo effect of an additional therapy has a strong influence on the benefit received.

PHYSIOTHERAPY

This is one of the longest tested treatments used in injuries and after surgery on the limbs. Chartered physiotherapists and veterinary nurses who have studied the subject work under the direction of the vet who is ready to advise or apply procedures that will help mobility and recovery.

Massage, heat, exercise or electrical stimulation are used to

The selection of healthy breeding stock is key to preventing the occurrence of inherited diseases.

relieve pain, regain movement and restore muscle strength.

HYDROTHERAPY

This is a popular therapy, as Cockers enjoy the use of water for the treatment of joint disease, injuries, or for the maintenance of fitness and health.

ACUPUNCTURE

This therapy has a long history of healing derived from Chinese medicine, involving the insertion of fine needles into specific locations in the body known as 'acupuncture points'.

The placing of the needles to stimulate nervous tissue is based on human charts, and very good results have been reported when veterinary acupuncturists have been allowed to select suitable cases to treat.

REIKI

This involves the laying on of the therapist's hands, and can have beneficial results. The advantage is that it does not involve the dog tolerating needles in his body, but, to date, there are few qualified veterinary operators.

MAGNETIC THERAPY

This therapy is perhaps more questionable in observed results. It involves magnetic products that are applied to the dog to relieve pain and increase mobility.

AROMATHERAPY

This involves treating dogs with remedies that they would once have found in the wild. It involves the use of selected essential oils and plant extracts.

If you take good care of your Cocker Spaniel, you will be rewarded with years of happy companionship.

PHYTOTHERAPY OR HERBAL MEDICINE

This has proven benefits, and there are an ever-increasing number of veterinary surgeons skilled in selecting appropriate plant products. Natural remedies are attractive to many users and provide a good alternative to a good number of conventional veterinary treatments.

Herbal drugs have become increasingly popular and their use is widespread, but licensing regulations and studies on interactions between herbal products and other veterinary medicines are still incomplete. Often a complex mixture of herbs will be prescribed, and it is not always clear which ones are effective. For example, a prescription for skin disease might include Calendula officinalis (marigold flower) for its antimicrobial, antifungal effects, Echinacea spp. (coneflower root) as an antimicrobial and immune stimulant, Rehmannia glutinosa (rehmannia root) as an anti-inflammatory, antiallergic and 'blood tonic', Valeriana officinalis (valerian root) as a nerve sedative, Taraxacum officinale (dandelion root) as a liver stimulant and laxative, Urtica dioica (nettle leaf) for its antihistamine effect, and Glycyrrhiza glabra (liquorice root) as another anti-inflammatory.

As with all alternative therapies, you need to consult a person who has the experience and specialist knowledge of applying the treatments. The Cocker's own vet should be informed, since some veterinary medicines should not be used when other remedies are involved.

THE CONTRIBUTORS

THE EDITOR: DEREK SHAPLAND (DERACOR)

Derek and his wife Coral have been breeding and showing Cocker Spaniels since 1976 under the Deracor affix. They have had some continued success in the ring, having won CCs with two different dogs. Derek had been the Secretary of the West of England Cocker Spaniel Club for 15 years, retiring from this post in 2004. Two years ago he was elected to the post of Secretary of the national parent club, The Cocker Spaniel Club. He has been judging Cocker Spaniels at Championship shows since 1991, and has officiated both at home and overseas.
See Chapter One: Getting To Know Cocker Spaniels, and Chapter Seven: The Perfect Cocker.

JANE SIMMONDS (SHENMORE)

Jane and her husband Andrew have been breeding and showing parti-coloured Cocker Spaniels under the Shenmore affix for more than 20 years, making up three Show Champions during this time. Jane has also offered a grooming service for Cockers for many years and helps run a busy Cocker internet forum dedicated to providing help and advice on all aspects of Cocker ownership.
See Chapter Three: A Cocker for your Lifestyle, Chapter Four: The New Arrival and Chapter Five: The Best of Care.

CAROL WEST (SHEIGRA)

Carol has owned Cockers for 26 years, and judges both at home and abroad. She has made up four Show Champions, and serves on various Cocker breed club committees. For about 15 years has been a breed rescue officer and helps to find suitable homes for abandoned, homeless or unwanted Cockers. An interest in the history of the breed led to her being appointed as Custodian for the newly formed Cocker Spaniel Club Memorabilia Collection. The aim of this is to collect old pedigrees, photographs and other historical items relating to the early years to preserve them for future generations to enjoy.
See Chapter Two: The First Cockers.

DICK LANE BSc, FRAgS, FRCVS

Dick qualified from the Royal Veterinary College in 1953 and then spent most of his time working in veterinary practice in Warwickshire. Over the years Dick developed a particular interest in assistance dogs: working for the Guide Dogs for the Blind Association and more recently for Dogs for the Disabled as a founder Trustee. Dick has been awarded a Fellowship of the Royal College of Veterinary Surgeons and a Fellowship of the Royal Agricultural Societies. He has recently completed an Honours BSc in Applied Animal Behaviour and Training, awarded by the University of Hull.
See Chapter Eight: Happy and Healthy.

JULIA BARNES

Julia has owned and trained a number of different dog breeds, and she is also a puppy socialiser for Dogs for the Disabled. A former journalist, she has written many books, including several on dog training and behaviour. Julia is indebted to Coral Shapland for breed-specific information on training and behaviour.
See Chapter Six: Training and Socialisation.

Derek Shapland with Deracor Deliverance

Jane Simmonds with Shenmore Sunny Jim.

Carol West with (back row, left to right): Sheigra Sunrise, Sheigra Shamrock, Sheigra Sweet Simplicity, Sh. Ch. Sheigra Swinging Sixties JW; (front row, left to right): Sh. Ch. Sheigra Starshine JW and Sh. Ch. Sheigra Special Vintage JW.

USEFUL ADDRESSES

KENNEL & BREED CLUBS

UK

The Kennel Club
1 Clarges Street, London, W1J 8AB
Tel: 0870 606 6750
Fax: 0207 518 1058
Web: www.the-kennel-club.org.uk

To obtain up-to-date contact information for the following breed clubs, please contact the Kennel Club:
• The Cocker Spaniel Club
• Cheshire Cocker Spaniel Club
• Cocker Spaniel Club of Lancashire
• Cocker Spaniel Club of Scotland
• Coventry Cocker Spaniel Club
• Devon and Cornwall Cocker Spaniel Club
• East Anglian Cocker Spaniel Society
• East of Scotland Cocker Spaniel Club
• Hampshire and Sussex Cocker Spaniel Club
• Home Counties Cocker Spaniel Club
• London Cocker Spaniel Society
• Midland Cocker Spaniel Club
• North Midlands and Eastern Counties Cocker Spaniel Club
• North of England Cocker Spaniel Association
• North of Ireland Cocker Spaniel Club
• North Wales Cocker Spaniel Club
• Parti-coloured Cocker Spaniel Club
• Rotherham and District Cocker Spaniel Club
• Solid Colours Cocker Spaniel Association
• South Wales and Monmouthshire Cocker Spaniel Club
• Ulster Cocker Spaniel Club
• West of England Cocker Spaniel Club
• Yorkshire Cocker Spaniel Club

USA

American Kennel Club (AKC)
5580 Centerview Drive,
Raleigh, NC 27606, USA.
Tel: 919 233 9767
Fax: 919 233 3627
Email: info@akc.org
Web: www.akc.org

United Kennel Club (UKC)
100 E Kilgore Rd, Kalamazoo,
MI 49002-5584, USA.
Tel: 269 343 9020
Fax: 269 343 7037
Web:www.ukcdogs.com/

English Cocker Spaniel Club of America, Inc.
Web: http://www.ecsca.org/

For contact details of regional clubs, please contact the English Cocker Spaniel Club of America.

AUSTRALIA

Australian National Kennel Council (ANKC)
The Australian National Kennel Council is the administrative body for pure breed canine affairs in Australia. It does not, however, deal directly with dog exhibitors, breeders or judges. For information pertaining to breeders, clubs or shows, please contact the relevant State or Territory Controlling Body.

Dogs Australian Capital Teritory
PO Box 815, Dickson ACT 2602
Tel: (02) 6241 4404
Fax: (02) 6241 1129
Email: administrator@dogsact.org.au
Web: www.dogsact.org.au

Dogs New South Wales
PO Box 632, St Marys, NSW 1790
Tel: (02) 9834 3022 or 1300 728 022 (NSW Only)
Fax: (02) 9834 3872
Email: info@dogsnsw.org.au
Web: www.dogsnsw.org.au

Dogs Northern Territory
PO Box 37521, Winnellie NT 0821
Tel: (08) 8984 3570
Fax: (08) 8984 3409
Email: admin@dogsnt.com.au
Web: www.dogsnt.com.au

Dogs Queensland
PO Box 495, Fortitude Valley Qld 4006
Tel: (07) 3252 2661
Fax: (07) 3252 3864
Email: info@dogsqueensland.org.au
Web: www.dogsqueensland.org.au

Dogs South Australia
PO Box 844
Prospect East SA 5082
Tel: (08) 8349 4797
Fax: (08) 8262 5751
Email: info@dogssa.com.au
Web: www.dogssa.com.au

Tasmanian Canine Association Inc
The Rothman Building
PO Box 116
Glenorchy Tas 7010
Tel: (03) 6272 9443
Fax: (03) 6273 0844
Email: tca@iprimus.com.au
Web: www.tasdogs.com

Dogs Victoria
Locked Bag K9
Cranbourne VIC 3977
Tel: (03)9788 2500
Fax: (03) 9788 2599
Email: office@dogsvictoria.org.au
Web: www.dogsvictoria.org.au

Dogs Western Australia
PO Box 1404
Canning Vale WA 6970
Tel: (08) 9455 1188
Fax: (08) 9455 1190
Email: k9@dogswest.com
Web: www.dogswest.com

INTERNATIONAL

Fédération Cynologique Internationalé (FCI)/World Canine Organisation
Place Albert 1er, 13, B-6530 Thuin, Belgium.
Tel: +32 71 59.12.38
Fax: +32 71 59.22.29
Web: www.fci.be/

TRAINING AND BEHAVIOUR

UK

Association of Pet Dog Trainers
PO Box 17, Kempsford, GL7 4WZ
Telephone: 01285 810811
Email: APDToffice@aol.com
Web: http://www.apdt.co.uk

Association of Pet Behaviour Counsellors
PO BOX 46, Worcester, WR8 9YS
Telephone: 01386 751151
Fax: 01386 750743
Email: info@apbc.org.uk
Web: http://www.apbc.org.uk/

USA

Association of Pet Dog Trainers
101 North Main Street, Suite 610
Greenville, SC 29601, USA.
Tel: 1 800 738 3647
Email: information@apdt.com
Web: www.apdt.com/

American College of Veterinary Behaviorists
College of Veterinary Medicine, 4474 Tamu, Texas A&M University
College Station, Texas 77843-4474
Web: http://dacvb.org/

American Veterinary Society of Animal Behavior
Web: www.avsabonline.org/

AUSTRALIA

APDT Australia Inc
PO Box 3122, Bankstown Square, NSW 2200.
Email: secretary@apdt.com.au
Web: www.apdt.com.au

Canine Behaviour
For details of regional behvaiourists, contact the relevant State or Territory Controlling Body.

ACTIVITIES

UK
Agility Club
http://www.agilityclub.co.uk/

British Flyball Association
PO Box 990, Doncaster, DN1 9FY
Telephone: 01628 829623
Email: secretary@flyball.org.uk
Web: http://www.flyball.org.uk/

Working Trials
36 Elwyndene Road, March, Cambridgeshire,
    PE15 9RL.
www.workingtrials.co.uk

USA
North American Dog Agility Council
P.O. Box 1206, Colbert,
OK 74733, USA.
Web: www.nadac.com/

North American Flyball Association, Inc.
1333 West Devon Avenue, #512
Chicago, IL 60660
Tel/Fax: 800 318 6312
Email: flyball@flyball.org
Web: www.flyball.org/

AUSTRALIA
Agility Dog Association of Australia
ADAA Secretary, PO Box 2212,
Gailes, QLD 4300, Australia.
Tel: 0423 138 914
Email: admin@adaa.com.au
Web: www.adaa.com.au/

**NADAC Australia (North American Dog
Agility Council - Australian Division)**
12 Wellman Street, Box Hill South, Victoria
3128, Australia.
Email: shirlene@nadacaustralia.com
Web: www.nadacaustralia.com/

Australian Flyball Association
PO Box 4179, Pitt Town, NSW 2756
Tel: 0407 337 939
Email: info@flyball.org.au
Web: www.flyball.org.au/

INTERNATIONAL
World Canine Freestyle Organisation
P.O. Box 350122, Brooklyn, NY 11235-2525,
USA
Tel: (718) 332-8336
Fax: (718) 646-2686
Email: wcfodogs@aol.com
Web: www.worldcaninefreestyle.org

HEALTH

UK
Alternative Veterinary Medicine Centre
Chinham House, Stanford in the Vale,
Oxfordshire, SN7 8NQ
Tel: 01367 710324
Fax: 01367 718243
Web: www.alternativevet.org/

British Small Animal Veterinary Association
Woodrow House, 1 Telford Way,
Waterwells Business Park, Quedgeley,
Gloucestershire, GL2 2AB
Tel: 01452 726700
Fax: 01452 726701
Email: customerservices@bsava.com
Web: http://www.bsava.com/

Royal College of Veterinary Surgeons
Belgravia House, 62-64 Horseferry Road,

London, SW1P 2AF
Tel: 0207 222 2001
Fax: 0207 222 2004
Email: admin@rcvs.org.uk
Web: www.rcvs.org.uk

USA
**American Holistic Veterinary Medical
Association**
2218 Old Emmorton Road
Bel Air, MD 21015
Tel: 410 569 0795
Fax 410 569 2346
Email: office@ahvma.org
Web: www.ahvma.org/

American Veterinary Medical Association
1931 North Meacham Road, Suite 100,
Schaumburg, IL 60173-4360, USA.
Tel: 800 248 2862
Fax: 847 925 1329
Web: www.avma.org

American College of Veterinary Surgeons
19785 Crystal Rock Dr, Suite 305
Germantown, MD 20874, USA.
Tel: 301 916 0200
Toll Free: 877 217 2287
Fax: 301 916 2287
Email: acvs@acvs.org
Web: www.acvs.org/

AUSTRALIA
Australian Holistic Vets
Web: www.ahv.com.au/

**Australian Small Animal Veterinary
Association**
40/6 Herbert Street, St Leonards, NSW 2065,
Australia.
Tel: 02 9431 5090
Fax: 02 9437 9068
Email: asava@ava.com.au
Web: www.asava.com.au

Australian Veterinary Association
Unit 40, 6 Herbert Street, St Leonards, NSW
2065, Australia.
Tel: 02 9431 5000
Fax: 02 9437 9068
Web: www.ava.com.au

Australian College Veterinary Scientists
Building 3, Garden City Office Park,
2404 Logan Road, Eight Mile Plains,
Queensland 4113, Australia.
Tel: 07 3423 2016
Fax: 07 3423 2977
Email: admin@acvs.org.au
Web: http://acvsc.org.au

ASSISTANCE DOGS

Canine Partners
Mill Lane, Heyshott, Midhurst,
, GU29 0ED
Tel: 08456 580480
Fax: 08456 580481
Web: www.caninepartners.co.uk

Dogs for the Disabled
The Frances Hay Centre, Blacklocks Hill,
Banbury, Oxon, OX17 2BS
Tel: 01295 252600
Web: www.dogsforthedisabled.org

Guide Dogs for the Blind Association
Burghfield Common, Reading, RG7 3YG
Tel: 01189 835555
Fax: 01189 835433
Web: www.guidedogs.org.uk/

Hearing Dogs for Deaf People
The Grange, Wycombe Road, Saunderton,
Princes Risborough, Bucks, HP27 9NS
Tel: 01844 348100
Fax: 01844 348101
Web: www.hearingdogs.org.uk

Pets as Therapy
3a Grange Farm Cottages, Wycombe Road,
Saunderton, Princes Risborough,
Bucks, HP27 9NS
Tel: 01845 345445
Fax: 01845 550236
Web: http://www.petsastherapy.org/

Support Dogs
21 Jessops Riverside, Brightside Lane,
Sheffield, S9 2RX
Tel: 01142 617800
Fax: 01142 617555
Email: supportdogs@btconnect.com
Web: www.support-dogs.org.uk

USA
Therapy Dogs International
88 Bartley Road, Flanders, NJ 07836,.
Tel: 973 252 9800
Fax: 973 252 7171
Email: tdi@gti.net
Web: www.tdi-dog.o

Therapy Dogs Inc.
P.O. Box 20227, Cheyenne, WY 82003.
Tel: 307 432 0272.
Fax: 307-638-2079
Web: www.therapydogs.com

Delta Society - Pet Partners
875 124th Ave NE, Suite 101 • Bellevue, WA
98005 USA.
Email: info@DeltaSociety.org
Web: www.deltasociety.org

Comfort Caring Canines
8135 Lare Street, Philadelphia, PA 19128.
Email: ccc@comfortcaringcanines.org
Web: www.comfortcaringcanines.org/

AUSTRALIA
AWARE Dogs Australia, Inc
PO Box 883, Kuranda, Queensland, 488,
Australia.
Tel: 07 4093 8152
Web: www.awaredogs.org.au/

Delta Society –- Therapy Dogs
Web: www.deltasociety.com.au